HE[...]
Guide's Greatest
ANGEL STORIES

REVIEW AND HERALD® PUBLISHING ASSOCIATION
HAGERSTOWN, MD 21740

The authors assume full responsibility for the accuracy of all facts
and quotations as cited in this book.

All Scripture references are from the *Holy Bible, New
International Version*. Copyright © 1973, 1978, 1984, International
Bible Society. Used by permission of Zondervan Bible Publishers.

This book was
Edited by Helen Lee Robinson
Cover designed by Trent Truman
Cover art by Tim Jessell
Typeset: 13/16 Goudy

PRINTED IN U.S.A.

09 08 07 06 05   5 4 3 2 1

R&H Cataloging Service
Guide's greatest angel stories,
    Compiled and edited by Helen Lee

    1. Angels—Stories.   I. Robinson, Helen Lee, 1976-   .

                    242

ISBN 0-8280-1880-4

Contents

Also by Helen Lee Robinson:

Guide's Greatest Christmas Stories
Guide's Greatest Escape From Crime Stories
Guide's Greatest Miracle Stories
Guide's Greatest Prayer Stories
Guide's Greatest Sabbath Stories

To order, call 1-800-765-6955.

Visit us at www.reviewandherald.com for information on other Review and Herald® products.

A special thanks to the authors we were unable to locate. If anyone can provide knowledge of their current mailing address, please relay this information to Helen Lee Robinson, in care of the Review and Herald® Publishing Association, 55 West Oak Ridge Drive, Hagerstown, Maryland 21740.

Introduction

"Not until the providences of God are seen in the light of eternity shall we understand what we owe to the care and interposition of His angels. Celestial beings have taken an active part in the affairs of men. They have appeared in garments that shone as the lightning; they have come as men, in the garb of wayfarers. They have accepted the hospitalities of human homes; they have acted as guides to benighted travelers. They have thwarted the spoiler's purpose and turned aside the stroke of the destroyer" (Ellen G. White, *Education*, pp. 304, 305).

We read stories in the Bible of angels appearing to people such as Abraham, Daniel, Mary, and Peter. But are angels still concerned about human beings today? I believe so! And although we may not always be able to see them at work, we can know that they are there.

I hope you enjoy these exciting angel stories from *Guide* (a weekly Christian magazine for young people). And remember: angels are watching over you!

—Helen Lee Robinson

1

Through Deep Waters

by Inez Storie Carr

Kem was surrounded by a circle of belligerent dog eyes. Whenever he shifted his body by the slightest movement to ease the pinching of the chains or the tightness of the ropes, the circle of dogs growled, tensing their muscles.

Kem knew that any attempt to escape would be futile. There was no way to get past the trained dogs. Besides, escape would be impossible anyway, for the bandits had bound him up like a package of meat in ropes and chains. They wanted to be sure he did not get away from them until they were ready to dispose of him in their own savage way.

Kem was an innocent Chinese boy from the Seventh-day Adventist mission who was being held for ransom. Kem knew about bandits. Ever since he was young he had heard stories of their dark deeds and knew better than to expect any mercy at their hands. He knew that at any moment they could decide to kill him. *If only they will give me a quick death,* his thoughts repeated mechanically again and again.

Kem was a Christian who had learned to look beyond Earth's darkest situations to heaven above. As his prayers ascended to the God he had learned to love and obey, his heart felt strengthened to face the death that now seemed inevitable.

Suddenly a fine looking young man appeared before him. Kem glanced at the dogs, expecting them to go into a frenzy and tear the young man to pieces. Instead, they were still watching him as though nothing unusual was taking place. They seemed to neither see nor hear what was going on.

The stranger walked up to the helpless boy and began undoing the ropes and chains. The dogs still did not move.

The story of Peter held between armed guards flashed into Kem's mind as the kind stranger said, "Follow me." Kem followed and walked right past the dogs. The dogs still had not noticed that something unusual was taking place.

Kem and the young man walked briskly until they came to a river. Again the stranger said, "Follow me," as he began to wade into the river. It was a deep river, with a deeper channel running through its center. The water in the shallow part came up to Kem's knees, and he wondered how he would ever walk through the deep part, but he kept on anyway.

It was a test of faith Kem would never forget. Although he waded across the river, through the deepest part of the channel, the water never came above his knees.

When they were on the other side of the river, the stranger pointed to a path that led toward the hills. "Follow this path," he said.

Kem started walking and suddenly found himself alone on the winding trail. He walked and walked, following the path. He had no idea where he was headed, but he obediently kept on as he had been instructed.

Later that day Kem walked right into the Seventh-day Adventist conference headquarters in China. He told the story to elder S. G. White (who was then working in the Chinese Mission and later served as secretary to Ellen G. White). Elder White told the story to Elder E. M. Sears, and Elder Sears told it to me. And now I'm telling it to you, so that you may know that you have a friend you may appeal to at any time—your very own guardian angel.

2

The Man in the Brown Coat

by V. E. Robinson

It was a cold winter day in January 1940. The car was barely creeping along the slippery road, and the windshield wipers were failing to keep the window clear of the snow that was falling thick and fast. Time and again the Thomas family had to stop the car and brush off the snow. It was nearly dark when the family finally reached the station in London.

The Thomas family were missionaries in Kenya, East Africa. They had been on furlough for a year and were now heading back to Kenya. During that fateful year, World War II had begun. And although no bombs had fallen on England, many ships had been sunk in the waters surrounding the country.

Because it was dangerous to travel from England by sea, the missionary family had decided to take a train to the channel port of Folkestone, and from there cross to France. Then they would travel to Italy by train, where they would take a neutral ship to Mombasa, Africa.

Pastor and Mrs. Thomas and their four sons, ranging in ages from 3 to 13, stood in the pitch blackness of the railway station, holding their suitcases and waiting for the train to come. Because enemy planes could be flying overhead, no lights were permitted in public places. The blackout was taken very seriously.

Soon the Thomas family heard, rather than saw, the train come to a stop in front of them. Tightly holding hands, they boarded the train. Hundreds of soldiers also climbed aboard. The doors slammed, the guard blew his whistle, and the train slowly made its way out of the station.

How strange it felt to be riding along in the pitch blackness of the night! Conversations were going on all around them, but not a soul could they see. Slowly the minutes passed, the rails clicking off the miles as the train neared the seacoast where the steamer was waiting to take them across the English Channel to France. The Thomas boys peered out the window, but there were no lights from farmhouses nor from any of the villages they passed through. Even the ground, covered with snow though it was, was almost invisible in the dark.

After what seemed like hours, the train began to slow down, and then stopped. Hundreds of people poured out onto the platform, the Thomas family among them. But where were they to go? They stood bewildered in the icy wind.

Suddenly a tall man appeared out of the darkness. "Follow me," he said. "I know where you must go."

They followed him down the platform, through one door and then another into a room that was well lit. They stood there for a moment, blinking until their eyes adjusted to the light. Then they saw that this was the room where passports were examined and luggage inspected.

Their guide—a tall man dressed in a heavy brown overcoat—led them to a nearby table where an officer sat. The officer looked at their passports and then asked if they were carrying any letters.

"Yes, we are," Pastor Thomas admitted.

Because of the war, all mail leaving or entering England was carefully examined to see that no important information was going out that might help the enemy countries. Pastor Thomas laid the letters on the table. They were letters written by former missionaries to their African friends in Kenya. The letters were written in an African language. This was very serious because there was no one in the room who could read and translate the letters except Pastor Thomas himself, and the officer would not agree to that.

Just then the man in the brown coat spoke up. "They are missionaries," he said. "I know them, and I know that there is nothing in those letters dangerous to the country."

"Very well," said the officer. "We will let them pass."

Pastor Thomas looked at the stranger in surprise. Where had this man met their family before? How could he know what was in the letters? It was very mysterious. Pastor Thomas thanked the man, who then proceeded to help out in another difficulty.

All over the room customs officers were examining luggage. They were taking no chances. One of the officers approached the Thomas family and asked them to open their luggage for inspection. The suitcases had been tightly strapped, and the idea of opening them was disheartening.

The man in the brown coat spoke up again. "These people are missionaries," he told the inspector. "I can vouch for their luggage. It does not contain anything prohibited by law."

"Very well," said the officer, and he waved them toward the door leading to the gangplank.

A few minutes later the family had climbed onto the ship. Dim lights were burning in the interior. One of the stewards came forward and explained that nearly all the beds on board had been taken by the soldiers, but he did have a few places for the ladies. He asked Mrs. Thomas to follow him, but she declined. She wanted to stay with her family. If the ship were torpedoed, at least the family would all go down together. The steward shrugged his shoulders and went on his way.

Almost instinctively Pastor Thomas turned to the man in the brown coat who had led them onto the boat. He did not fail them. "I know a place for you. It is not an ideal place for a missionary family to sleep, but at least you will not be disturbed," he said.

He led them to the ship's bar. It was after midnight, and the bar was closed. Around the room by the wall were leather-padded benches. The family could lie down on them and rest for the remainder of the night.

Pastor Thomas pushed the suitcases under the benches and turned to thank the tall stranger once again for all his kindness, but he was gone. Pastor Thomas stepped into the hall and looked up and down the passage. Not a sign of him could he see. He asked the officers at the top of the gangplank if they had seen where the man in the brown coat had gone.

"There wasn't anyone like that on the boat tonight," they said. "Otherwise, we would have seen him."

But Pastor Thomas knew there had been such a man, for he had talked to him. But now he had disappeared, totally, completely, into the night.

"It must have been an angel," said Mrs. Thomas softly.

3

Angel on Front Street

by Ivy R. Doherty

We'd better head to the train station," Jane's father called as he appeared in the farmhouse doorway. He reached down and picked up Jane's suitcase and a basket of food for Aunt Ellen. "Kiss Mother and let's be gone."

Jane made the rounds of the family with her goodbyes. There were five younger children holding their faces up to be kissed. Their oldest sister would be gone for only three weeks to visit their aunt, but to the children, who loved their sister, this seemed like an eternity.

"There's Father tooting the car horn," Mother warned. "You must not miss your train. Now, Jane, please be careful in the city. Don't speak to strangers, and remember to conduct yourself as Father and I have taught you. Then you should be just fine."

"You don't need to worry, Mother. Aunt Ellen promised that Reggie and Ken would be at the station to meet me when I arrive."

The car whisked away in a whirl of dust, and with the barking of dogs and children's last shouted goodbyes Jane was gone.

Once on board the train, Jane settled down on a seat by a window to watch the farms and fields flash swiftly by. When she grew tired of watching she read awhile, then dozed.

Darkness had fallen by the time the train pulled in at its destination. Jane looked out the window expecting to wave a greeting to her cousins, who should have been waiting for her under the second platform light, but there was no Reggie and there was no Ken!

What if they don't come? Jane wondered as she stepped off the train. *Oh, that's a foolish thought. They'll be here.*

Jane carried her basket and suitcase to a seat on the platform where the boys would be sure to see her when they arrived. No doubt they had been delayed and would appear at any moment.

But as the minutes ticked away on the old station clock, fear clutched Jane's heart. *Something must have happened to the boys,* Jane thought. *Aunt Ellen would never let them be as late as this.*

What could she do? She did not have enough money in her pocket to hire a taxi, and she dared not count on getting money from Aunt Ellen to pay the driver; she might arrive at the house to find no one home. Nor could she phone Aunt Ellen; telephones were not as common then as they are now.

Jane shivered. Her stomach seemed as if it were turning upside down.

Ten more minutes. Still no boys. The longer she waited, the fainter grew her hope and courage. *I have to do something,* she finally decided. *I can't sleep at the station all night. I'll just have to walk to Aunt Ellen's.*

Out on the street she looked around. The place should have been familiar enough, but everything looked different now as she stood alone, feeling like a very small person in a very big and foreboding world. For the first time in her life she was on a city street all alone and at night. Jane wondered why the train station had to be in the gloomiest, wickedest-looking part of town. Gruff men stood around on the sidewalks and lingered in dim alleyways.

As she tried to muster up enough courage to venture out through the ugliness of it all, a drunken man approached her, staggering as he came. Jane knew she must get out of this horrible nightmare at all costs. She picked up her feet and began to move down the street.

With each step she took, her feet felt like they were weighted with lead. Evil stares and smirking smiles chilled her. Then all at once she remembered that this was family worship time in her home. Perhaps Mother was praying for her right now. "Oh, God," Jane cried in her heart, "get me out of this awful place. Please send angels to watch over me."

Unexpectedly and seemingly from nowhere, a clean-shaven, well-dressed young man stood before the bewildered Jane.

"You have a heavy basket there, young lady," he said with a smile.

As Jane looked into his face, she saw that it was gentle and good. Surprise filled her heart in place of the fears that had been crowding there. What would such a person be doing, lingering here on Front Street?

"Would you allow me to carry your basket?" he asked Jane kindly.

Now Jane was frightened again. What should she do? She forced herself to speak. "No, thank you," she said. "I am perfectly all right, and I can manage."

Without another word the young man walked ahead of Jane, a few yards in front of her.

Will he never leave me alone? Jane wondered in fright after they had gone two or three blocks this way. She prayed at every step. Then they were out of Front Street, moving toward the better section of town, where Aunt Ellen lived.

Sometimes the kind young man was silent. Sometimes he hummed a little tune, which seemed a sweeter melody than Jane had ever heard. Gradually her frightened spirits relaxed. Perhaps this was the way God was answering her prayer. Perhaps He had put it into the heart of this young man to see her safely home. The basket grew heavier and heavier with each step. Perhaps it would have been safe for her to trust him with it after all.

And now they were on Aunt Ellen's street. They came to her gate. The young man turned briefly to face Jane once more; then suddenly he was no longer there. Jane stared about her in the light that the street lamp cast. She could scarcely believe that the street was deserted, and yet her escort had certainly disappeared completely.

Realization of what had happened dawned on her mind. God had indeed answered her prayer and had literally sent an angel as she had asked, for how could a human being have appeared and vanished as this being had done? Jane remembered the kind and gentle face. She would remember it as long as she lived.

It was late at night when Jane was awakened by Aunt Ellen and the boys. They had been called urgently from town not long before Jane's train was due to arrive. They had been very anxious for Jane's safety and were greatly relieved when they found her in bed sleeping.

"I'm glad you have a secret hiding place for your house key, Aunt Ellen," Jane said, laughing. "I wouldn't have been very comfortable sleeping on the front door mat!"

Then Jane remembered the wonder and happiness that had come to her from trusting God through her nightmare experience, and of course, she had to tell Aunt Ellen and the boys the whole story.

She slept soundly that night knowing that God looks after His children when they are in trouble.

4

Grandpa's Angel Guide

by Sylvia Lee

A stride his dapple-gray Chinese pony, Grandpa entered a small town about four days journey from his destination, Chengtu, the capital of the largest province in China. He stopped in front of the post office, dismounted, tied the horse to a post, and entered to ask for his mail.

"Is there mail for Pastor Wong Ho Ren?" he asked the man behind the window.

Yes, there were letters addressed to him both in his Chinese name and in his English name—M. C. Warren. Letters from home! It was always a comfort on these long, lonely trips to receive letters from his family. (Of course, Grandpa was not a grandfather yet. In fact, my mother was one of his three small daughters at that time.)

As he turned to leave the post office and catch up

to his luggage carriers and cook boy, a Chinese gentleman stepped up and asked, "Are you a Seventh-day Adventist?"

Smiling warmly in his friendly manner Grandpa answered, "Why, yes, I am. How did you know?"

"Well, I happened to see the return address on your letters," he answered. "I would like to ask you some questions about your religion."

"I'd be glad to answer any questions you have to ask me," offered Grandpa, for it was always a joy to him to tell others about the Bible.

After a lengthy talk at the gentleman's home, the man ask, "What hotel are you staying in tonight?"

"I'm not staying here tonight," Grandpa answered. "I plan to go on to Gindaipu [Golden Girdle Village]."

"Gindaipu!" exclaimed the man. "You can't make it there before dark!"

"Why not? Isn't it only 15 *li* [about five miles] from here?"

"No, it is 40 *li* from here. You shouldn't plan on going on tonight."

"But I must. My luggage carriers and my baggage have all gone ahead."

Grandpa bid the man goodbye and hastened out of the town and onto the road alone. His two-hour delay had put many *li* between him and his carriers.

He covered 20 *li* before dark and stopped at a small village to inquire whether his carriers had passed through. Finding that they had, he entered a small shop to buy a paper lantern. The first three lanterns were so flimsy that they fell apart when a candle was put into them. Finally he found one that would hold a candle.

Fear gripped his heart as he started alone and un-armed up the mountain in the dark. As he breathed a prayer for protection and guidance, Grandpa's fear gradually went away.

Alas! The candle in his lantern lasted only till he was at the top of the first ridge. He had a spare can-dle but no way to light it. He hadn't anticipated the wind blowing out his first candle.

On the long descent to the ravine below, Grandpa decided it would be safer to get off and lead the horse down the flagstone steps. Although travel-ing in the dark was slow, the thought occurred to him that it had its advantages—at least he could not be observed by lurking foes as easily as he would have been with a lighted lantern.

At the bottom of the hill there was a stone bridge that crossed a little stream. Grandpa noticed that about 30 steps up the incline from the bridge was a house, for he could see shafts of light coming through the cracks. The house was about 40 feet wide, and the middle section had a large double door, which opened as Grandpa drew near.

Two Chinese men emerged from the doorway. In

his best Chinese, Grandpa asked politely, "May I bother you to light my candle from yours?"

Willingly they lit the candle, and one of the men asked, "Where are you going?"

"Gindaipu," answered Grandpa.

"I'm also going to Gindaipu. We can travel together."

The man who had spoken looked good and honest, and Grandpa was relieved to have him go along with him, as robbers were known to be operating on this road.

With their lanterns in hand, Grandpa and the Chinese man started up the road. Grandpa deliberately kept the man talking as much as possible because he had a theory that if the bandits were local men, they would not rob someone from their own community.

"I'm glad to be able to go along with you," the Chinese man said. "It is dangerous on this road."

Why should he say that? thought Grandpa. *He doesn't have much to lose. All he has are grass sandals and plain cotton clothing. He probably has no money to lose at all. Here I have almost 40 silver dollars with me! I should be the one who's thankful for someone to go with!*

On they traveled many miles. Then, when they came to a path that led away from the main road, the Chinese man said, "I must go this way now. Goodbye."

"I thought you were going to Gindaipu," said

Grandpa, disappointed, for he had enjoyed the stranger's company.

"It is just a little way from here," the man answered. "From here on there is no more danger. I must go this way."

After watching his companion disappear into the darkness, Grandpa continued on the main road. Suddenly he came to a standstill as he saw a light—no, two lights—coming toward him! These were not paper and candle lanterns, but expensive kerosene lamps! It must be a group of men.

As the lights drew nearer Grandpa realized that the second light was only the reflection of the lantern in the water of the paddy fields. As the light drew still nearer, he saw with a sigh of relief that the "group of men" he had imagined was only one man.

Grandpa stepped aside to let the man pass. A tingle went down his spine as a hand reached through the darkness and took his horse's reins from him! Then he realized it was his faithful cook boy out searching for him.

Tired and weary, they came into Gindaipu. The innkeeper seemed greatly relieved when Grandpa arrived safely. He said a man had been robbed and seriously injured on that same road only a day or two before. That night Grandpa knelt beside his cot and thanked the Lord for taking care of him along the dangerous country road.

So where does the angel come into the story? Grandpa himself did not know till his return trip. Always endeavoring to make friends and renew acquaintances, he planned to stop at the house where he had gotten the light for his candle.

There was the stone bridge. And there about 30 steps above the road *should* have been the house. But there was no house! Furthermore, no house had ever been there! There was not even a leveled spot where a house could have stood! God had provided. He had sent an angel to be with him that night.

Grandpa recalled the words of the stranger: "I am glad to be able to go with you. It is dangerous to travel this road alone." He now realized that it had been not his own safety but Grandpa's that the traveler had been thinking of.

5

The Choir of Angels

by Ella M. Robinson

A re we going to camp meeting?" the children asked.

"How can we leave our homes and farms?" the hardworking fathers asked. "We can arrange for the care of the livestock, but if our crops are not harvested on time, there will be a serious loss. And we need all the money we can get to carry us through another winter."

"But there'll be special blessings for us at camp meeting. How can we afford to stay home?" the mothers asked.

For weeks the question was discussed by three families of poor struggling farmers in Nebraska. Ministers and churches were few in those early days, and the lack was partly supplied by the yearly camp meetings that were being held in many states.

Finally they decided to go and trust God with the results.

On the afternoon before the departure, the farm wagons were loaded with clothing and bedding and food. In the morning the mothers rose early to bake bread. Then, after prayers for a safe journey, men, women, and children climbed aboard.

And so, with some sitting on the driver's seat and others on boxes and bundles, the three families started off across the plains. In the heart of some of the older folks there lingered a prayer that God would take special care of their farms during their absence, but for the younger ones there was only joyful anticipation of the good times they would have at the meetings.

No one was disappointed. As old and young listened together day after day to the thrilling talks and Bible studies, many amens rose from the audience. No one talked of the sacrifices made in leaving homes and farms at this critical season.

On the return journey after the meetings, the party stopped to make camp for the night on the open prairie. What was that they heard? Singing? Yes! Sweet singing! Where did it come from? There were no people in sight except their little company. They could see for miles in every direction—not a tree or house, nothing but grass on every side. The singing seemed to come out of the air above them, and it was very near.

Camp making was halted. Everyone stood and listened in awed silence. The song was one they knew well—"Children of the heavenly King, as you journey sweetly sing."

At first some tried to join in but soon hushed their own voices, for they sounded harsh and unmusical compared with the melody and sweetness floating down from above. Every word was clear and plain.

The singers completed the song and started again with the first verse. Then the music became softer and seemed to be drifting away *as the choir of angels departed.*

Yes, they knew! God had honored those faithful farmers by sending heavenly visitors to comfort and cheer their hearts, and to help them realize how pleased their heavenly Provider was with them because they had been willing to risk financial loss in order to make the kingdom of heaven first of all.

6

The Mystery of the Cowardly Assassin

by Jan S. Doward

Evening had come to the Sumatran jungle, and the darkness seemed to settle into the very heart of everything. There was always some movement in the jungle at night, and the noises of the creatures that crept forth reminded one that the thickets were very much alive.

Missionary von Asselt and his wife would sit and read from the Word of God whenever they were frightened. Often there seemed to come from the surrounding jungle more than the noises of animals and wild birds. The screeching and crying seemed to haunt them at times, and always present was the fear of being murdered by the hostile men from the local tribe.

It was on such a night as this that the two were huddled together over the precious Book when they heard a noise outside. It was not the screaming of a wild beast or the cry of a disturbed bird, but the thrashing of brush as if a hundred madmen were rushing toward them.

Terror seized the missionary couple, and as they had done so many times before, they knelt before the Lord and pleaded for protection. Often at other times they had risen before dawn and prayed and studied the Word in order to get peace of mind. Tonight was no different from any other except that they sensed something peculiarly dreadful, something that seemed about to happen—but not quite.

Outside, a band of angry men were following a hired assassin toward the missionaries' hut. Many times before, these natives had tried to kill the two missionaries, but without success. In desperation they had met with a professional assassin and offered to pay him to do the job.

The assassin had laughed at the failures of the others. "I fear no God and no devil," he said.

It was no idle boast. He really didn't fear anything. He belonged to a special guild of men who went about killing anyone for a price.

Brandishing his long sword over his head, he advanced through the bush with a gleam in his eye, determined to kill the missionary couple regardless of what might come. The other men dropped behind to watch. Courageously the killer came within the yard. Then suddenly his face blanched. His proud arm, which had so often struck down victims, fell helpless at his side. Staring in disbelief at what he saw, he turned and raced back to the others, shouting, "Flee for your lives!"

Knowing nothing of what had taken place outside, Pastor von Asselt got up from his knees. "I feel better now," he told his wife.

Two years passed by without the missionaries' experiencing any more of those terrifying sensations. During that time they moved inland to a more civilized tribe, which received them more kindly. Here they built a small house, and life became more cheerful and pleasant.

One day an acquaintance from the first tribe came to visit Pastor von Asselt. The two talked together for some time, and then the man turned to the missionary.

"Tuan," he said slowly, "I would like to have a close look at your watchmen."

"My watchmen?" the missionary asked in surprise.

"Yes, your watchmen. The men you have stationed about your house at night to protect you."

"Oh, I have no watchmen. Only a little herdboy and a little cook are with me, and they would make very poor watchmen." The missionary laughed.

The man looked the missionary in the eye as if to say, "Don't try to fool me. I know you have watchmen and are just trying to hide the fact."

"May I look through your house?" he asked.

The missionary consented. "You may look anywhere you wish."

The man looked in every corner of the small house, under the beds, and even between the sheets. Returning to the reception room, he sat down disappointed. "I know better. You have watchmen, but where are they?"

Von Asselt began asking questions, and the man told him of the many times the men of the tribe had banded together to kill him and his wife. Every time they had come to the house they had seen two rows of watchmen standing guard, and that had stopped them from carrying out their evil plan. The night they hired the assassin, they were sure they could get rid of the missionaries, for they hated them and were afraid of their religion.

"When the assassin came into your yard he saw the same two rows of men that we had seen before," the man explained. "He had been sure he could get through, but when he saw those strong men standing shoulder to shoulder with swords that glittered like fire he could not move forward but ran back. After that we never tried to harm you again. Now, Tuan, where are your watchmen?"

"I have never seen the watchmen," Von Asselt said.

"And your wife has never seen them?"

"No, my wife has never seen them."

"But all of us have seen them. How is that?"

Then Pastor von Asselt went to the shelf and picked up his Bible. Holding it in his hands he said, "See, here is the Word of our great God, in which He promises to guard and defend us. We firmly believe that Word. Therefore, we do not need to see the watchmen. You do not believe. Therefore, the great God has to show you the watchmen, in order that you may learn to believe."

7

Angels on Horseback

by Barbara Westphal

think we should stay in this village tonight," Emma said. "I don't want to walk back in the dark with this briefcase." She tugged at the heavy bag—heavy with pay for the books the girls had delivered that day. Emma had begun to sell books for a scholarship when she was only 14. Now, after two years in an Adventist academy in Central America, she was an experienced colporteur.

"I don't want to stay here tonight," declared her friend Irene. "I want to sleep in my own bed."

"It's too dangerous to walk an hour in the dark by ourselves with all this money," Emma said. "Oh, you're always so cautious! I'm not one bit scared."

"Haven't you noticed that a man has been following us most of the day?" asked Emma.

"You mean that polite fellow who is so interested in our work? Oh, he's just being friendly."

The man had been friendly, all right. Too friendly, Emma thought. He had asked if this was the day the girls were delivering books. The next time he met them he inquired if the girls were having good success collecting the money. And the next time he had even offered to accompany the girls back to the village where they were staying. How did he happen to meet them so often? Emma wondered. Well, maybe Irene was right. A polite, well-dressed gentleman like him surely couldn't be a thief.

No one likes to be a coward or to be laughed at so Emma gave in, and the two girls started out of the village. It was obvious that darkness would close down on them in a few minutes, for it was already twilight.

There was a long stretch of straight road and then a sharp turn. As the girls rounded the first curve, where they could no longer be seen from the village, they saw a man on horseback—the same man who had been so interested in their welfare.

"Give me that bag!" he demanded.

"No, it's not heavy," Emma replied evenly, pretending not to know they were being held up.

"This is no joke," the man snarled. "Give me that bag!"

The girls knew they couldn't put up much of a fight—and they saw a revolver in his belt. So they let him take the bag without resisting. Emma still tried to be polite. "Sir, everyone in town knows you are an honorable man. I'm sure you wouldn't take away from us what we have worked so hard to earn."

Even as she spoke, she had a sick feeling inside thinking of the loss of the 600 columbuses that would have paid for her and Irene to go back to school. How hard they had worked these last three months taking orders! She remembered the tired feet, the headaches, the hot sun, the missed meals. Was it all to be for nothing?

Suddenly two handsome policemen appeared on horseback, well armed. "Are you girls selling books?" they asked courteously. "Are you in trouble?"

"Yes," they sighed with relief, for the thief was already dropping their bag on the ground, putting spurs to his horse, and taking off.

Thankfully Emma picked up the precious brief-case and looked around to thank the two mounted policemen. They were nowhere to be seen! Yet the girls had not heard the hoofbeats of their horses on the ground! "Irene, have you ever seen mounted police before in our country?"

"No, I've never heard of policemen on horseback before, not around here, anyway."

Emma looked up and down the darkening road as she said reverently, "They weren't policemen. They were angels!"

8

Helpful Stranger

by Corrine Kandoll Vanderwerff

Margie pulled herself up onto her knees and peeped through the window above her bed. Already the morning was warm and dry. Only a few cloud puffs dented the sky as it promised another perfect summer day. She could see the sun shimmering off the tall greenness of the surrounding fields.

Turning from the window, she watched Blanche and Benny, her younger sister and brother, struggle with their last bit of sleep. "Up with you, you two sleepyheads," she teased. "Mother and Father and the others left for the field long ago, and we won't have any play time this morning if we don't hurry."

She slipped out of bed onto the rug that her mother used to cover the roughness of the cabin floor and pulled on her faded play dress. By that time the other two were out of bed. Margie dressed 3-year-old

Benny while Blanche struggled with her own clothes.

Soon they had finished the breakfast that their mother had left for them on the table. They set the dishes to soak, and Benny went outside to play while Blanche and Margie made the beds.

Finances were tight in those days, and jobs were hard to find. The Bliss family had found the answer to their needs by going to work in the fields. Life became one long camping trip for them. When work was finished in one place, Mother and Father would load their belongings into the trailer, pack their seven children into the car, and head for the next farm or orchard where work was available. At some places they had to live in a tent, but at other places, such as this one, they were provided with a cabin.

Each member of the family had his share of work to do. The four older children worked in the fields with their parents. Mrs. Bliss did not like to leave the three younger children by themselves during the day, but it was necessary; and Margie was getting to be quite a capable 7-year-old. Besides, there usually was a woman at home in one of the nearby cabins, and she was ready to help the children with any difficulties they might have.

This particular morning began like any other. Margie and Blanche were nearly finished making the beds. The plop-plop of the heavy quilts filled the cabin as the girls tried to shake the wrinkles out of them. Then there was a scream—not just a single scream, but one that continued, then wavered and built into a cry of increasing pain.

"Benny!" exclaimed the sisters running out of the cabin. The dust flew up between their bare toes as they dashed off the little porch and around the trailer parked beside the cabin.

Benny was grasping the top edge of the trailer sideboard. The whiteness showed around his fingernails as he tried to pull himself upward. But it was not his body that he was trying to lift; it was his foot. With each struggle to lift his foot higher, his cries increased. For every time he tried to lift his foot a board under it moved too.

"Here, Benny," Margie soothed, "sister will help you."

Carefully she tried to lift the little foot, but the nail held fast. She worked gently. Still it wouldn't budge. Finally, in desperation she placed both of her feet on the board and with her two hands she pulled on the foot. It began to slide loose from the nail—farther—farther—then it was free.

Margie gathered Benny into her arms. His screaming had quieted into sobs of pain. "You'd better get the neighbor lady," Margie told Blanche. "I don't know what to do to make Benny feel better."

Blanche ran to the neighbor's cabin. She banged on the door, but there was no answer.

"Oh, dear, what shall we do now?" Margie asked when Blanche returned alone.

"I wish Mother were here," Blanche remarked. She tried to comfort Benny, but her tears began to join his.

"I wish I knew where to find Mother and Father," said Margie. "All I know is that they are somewhere out there in that huge field with all those hundreds of other people. I don't even know which way to go to find them. I wish someone was here."

Soon Margie's tears joined those of the other two. And now that his sisters were crying, Benny began to cry louder again. Margie tried to fight back the tears and to comfort her brother, but she didn't know what to do or say. She only wished for someone to help her.

Just then a stranger dressed like one of the workers appeared from around the corner of the cabin. "Would you like me to get your mother for you?" he asked the tearful trio.

"Oh, yes. Please do," replied Margie, forcing back a sob.

After speaking a few words of comfort to the children, the man hurried off into the fields.

The thought that their parents would soon be coming cheered the children. Margie carried Benny inside and laid him on the bed. Then she got some water and tried to wash the dust off his hurt foot.

Meanwhile, the stranger walked into the field as if he had gone that way many times, straight toward a certain group of the workers. Approaching the group, he stepped up to the Blisses. "Sorry, folks," he said kindly, "but there's been a little accident back at camp. Your young son stepped on a nail. Don't worry, though; he'll be all right. But the children are alone and they need you." So saying, he continued on his way.

Mother and Father called their thanks after him and hurried to the cabin. Mother soaked Benny's foot in hot Epsom salts, and Father sent a message for the nurse to come by as soon as possible.

A while later the neighbor woman hurried over. "Oh, I'm so sorry I wasn't here," she apologized. "I went to town this morning, not thinking to tell you folks. The children always play so well, and nothing has ever happened before."

"This certainly was unexpected," replied Father Bliss. "I'm just glad that fellow happened along when he did. It's providential that he was in camp just the time he was."

After the excitement had died down, Margie was able to ask a question that had been on her mind. "Who was that nice man that went to get you?" she asked.

"I don't know," replied her father. "I've never seen him before. Didn't you tell him whom to get?"

Margie shook her head. "No, and he didn't even ask our names. He just came and said he'd get you for us."

Father looked thoughtful for a moment, and then

he said, "Yes, it was strange the way he came straight to us. He certainly was a kind man. I'd like to thank him again, whoever he is."

The family tried to find the stranger that day so they could give him their thanks again. They asked the others who had been working nearby if they knew anything about him. But no one knew who he was. No one had ever seen him before, and no one knew where he had gone. The camp was too far from a main road for a stranger to just happen to be passing through.

That evening when the family gathered for worship, Father took his Bible and turned to Psalm 34. He read only one verse, the seventh: "The angel of the Lord encamps around those who fear him, and he delivers them." Then he looked up from his Bible. "You know," he said, "God kept that promise today. Who else could have found us in that field without asking our names or even where we were working except an angel of the Lord? There is only One we can thank."

And so the family knelt and gave their thanks to God for sending His angel in their time of need.

9

The Angel in the Mine

by Amos Hash as told to Frances Shafer

In the year 1897 my brother and I bought a piece of land in Missouri to mine for lead and zinc. Already a 100-foot shaft had been sunk straight down through the rock, and a drift had been dug back into the earth at the 50-foot level. (A drift is a tunnel leading off the main mine shaft.) It was to this drift that I made my way on that never-to-be-forgotten day when I went down on *the new rope*.

I swung on the rope in the shaft, letting my hands slide until they should come to the knot where I wanted to get off. As I went lower and the full force of my weight pulled on the new rope, the rope began to unwind slowly.

New rope has many twists in it before it is well stretched. I didn't think of this fact that day, but the weight of my body was serving as a very good stretcher.

As I went lower, the rope unwound. It whirled me about as I came near the knot. I held on tightly, hoping it would stop its dizzy turning, but it pulled tighter and tighter, and whirled faster and faster, and soon I was spinning dizzily. I was down just 50 feet, and below me, 50 feet farther down, was solid rock.

Faster and faster I turned. My hands gripped tighter. They were getting sweaty, and my head was spinning and I could see nothing. That little knot was the only thing between me and the hard rock bottom. I could not see the drift opening at all, and I was powerless to save myself.

My brother was gone. My stomach was sick. My muscles cried for rest. Then my hands slipped.

"Oh, God," I cried, "save me!"

A hand reached out and drew me firmly by the shoulder into the open drift. When my feet touched the solid rock, I limply dropped the churning rope. A kind voice said, "You are sick, aren't you?" He led me to the wall, where I sat down upon the hard floor.

I lifted my eyes to my deliverer. I had never seen him before. He was a young man dressed in dark trousers and a clean, white shirt. I lowered my head for a moment because I was very weak and still dizzy, and then I raised my eyes to thank this new friend. He was gone.

There were two ways to reach that spot. One was the way I had come, and I knew he had not come that way. The other was through a narrow drift from another mine some 200 yards away. It was a very narrow, dirty tunnel. No clean, white shirt could have come through there unspotted.

10

The Man Just Disappeared

by Jill LeBaron

Gari Meier, her arms full of stovewood, pushed open the kitchen door and paused in surprise to see her mother standing at the sink washing the dishes. It had been a long time since Mother had been able to do that.

"How good it is to have you up, Mother!" Gari exclaimed, rushing over to give Mother a hug. Then she added with a mischievous smile, "And especially doing the dishes! It's just like old times, isn't it?"

"Yes, dear, it is. You'd be surprised how wonderful it seems just to be able to stand on my feet and put my hands in dishwater again. But you're not getting lazy in your old age, are you?" Mother teased.

Gari laughed. She hadn't had time to get lazy, but she did feel old sometimes. The responsibility of taking care of the house and her two younger brothers often weighed heavily on her teenage shoulders. Ever since the start of World War II her mother had been sick. The war had been going on now for almost two years, and that was just about how long her father had been gone, serving as a chaplain in the German Army.

Gari turned to gaze out the window. Things really had changed, she thought. How different their large beautiful farm in Eifel, Germany, had looked before the war. The leaves were coming out now in a bright spring green. The flowers were a bank of pink against the house, and wildflowers made blotches of white against the hillside and a flowing sea of yellow in the meadow. But, lovely as it was, the beauty of the season wasn't enough to console Gari. There was no singing from the birds, no crops in the fields, and no cattle in the pastures. She never saw her old friends nor even heard if they were safe.

Her thoughts brightened as she thought about how God had taken care of them. Look how the little garden beside the house had prospered and somehow escaped the notice of the soldiers who had tramped across their property several times that year. And with occasional help from her mother, she had canned more than enough vegetables last year, and it looked as if there would be plenty for them to put up this year too.

"Here, I'll finish the dishes," Gari offered suddenly, thinking that perhaps her mother wasn't strong enough yet to do that much.

"Really, Gari, I feel quite well this morning," Mother reassured her, then turned to question suddenly, "John, where do you think you're going?"

Gari's 12-year-old brother was passing through the kitchen toward the back door. Tim, his 7-year-old brother, was following behind.

"Just thought Tim and I would do a little exploring today," John explained.

"Do you think you should?" Mother asked with concern. "You know how dangerous the woods are. It hasn't been safe since the war started."

"But, Mother, we haven't heard guns for days. They've probably moved away by now."

Mother finally gave her consent, but a troubled look lingered on her face.

As Gari stood in the doorway watching her brothers walk toward the woods, she noticed how young they really were. "Lord, please protect them," she prayed and kept the prayer on her heart all day as she went about the housework.

The boys were not quite so serious-minded as they romped into the woods. "Let's go see if the T.R. is still there," Tim called, already on the run. T.R. was short for "tree ranch," which was what they called their tree house.

"There it is! There it is!" the two shouted in unison as they caught sight of their oversized hideaway, snuggled high in the fresh green branches of a large old tree. The miniature house had been made out of the lumber left over when the new barn had been built. Mr. Schultz, a carpenter who belonged to their church, had built it for them because of his appreciation for all that the boys' family had done for him.

"Looks like somebody's invaded the place," John observed anxiously after the boys had clambered up to the house.

"Yeah," agreed Tim as he surveyed the clutter all about the room. Then he noticed the wall. Bullets had carved splintery holes all along the back side. "Bullets!" he nearly shouted.

When they looked out the window to estimate just about where the bullets must have come from, something shiny, about 10 feet from the tree, caught their eye. Quickly they climbed down to see what it was.

"Hey, a bomb!" Tim exclaimed, his voice exploding with excitement.

"We'd better leave it here!" John cautioned, but he was already inspecting it eagerly.

"Something must be the matter with it if it fell all that way and didn't go off," Tim said. He had already made up his mind that the bomb couldn't be dangerous, and it would be such fun to play with. He began to tie a rope to one end of it in order to drag it home. His brother joined in.

Suddenly a man's voice made them jerk around. "Leave it alone, boys. It's dangerous." His tone was kind, but the words were firm and decisive. He stood tall and straight, and as calm as if there weren't a war at all, as if he were simply on a leisurely afternoon walk.

Something about the man made them obey immediately, and they scrambled to untie the rope. The simple task took only a minute, but when they turned around again, the man was gone. He had left without the slightest sound. The boys stared at the empty spot, then gazed intently around the deserted clearing.

They walked home in the late-afternoon sun, each absorbed in his own thoughts. Finally Tim interrupted the silence. "He just disappeared, John, didn't he? He just disappeared."

"People don't just disappear," John retorted. He tried to tell himself that the man must have gone somewhere.

As they neared home, Tim broke into a run. "Gari! Gari!" he shouted to their sister who was waiting for them in the doorway. When he got to her, his words spilled out. "We saw a man, and he just disappeared! He just disappeared."

A stranger in the woods? Gari's heart began to beat faster, and fear showed in her eyes. As least her brothers were safe, she thought as she said a silent prayer of thanks. The boys told her the rest of the story, and John kept repeating, "People don't just disappear. People don't just disappear."

The next day Gari and her brothers heard an explosion that seemed to rock the house. It could only mean that their bomb had exploded, for not one plane had been heard all day.

The boys rushed out of the house, anxious to see what it was all about. They reached the place of the explosion and saw the damage it had caused. As Gari looked around, she couldn't help thinking that her brothers could have been hurt or killed if it had not been for the man who had disappeared—the man sent from God.

The man sent from God? Could it be? Did God consider her brothers so precious that He'd sent an angel to protect them?

When Gari's father returned home a few months later, he answered her question. "If God loved us enough to send His only Son to save us," he told her, "He certainly considers each of us very precious. He has promised to care for all who put their trust in Him."

11

Angel Tracks

by Virginia Legg

O ld Man Winter had hung up his hat, apparently planning a prolonged visit in midwestern Wisconsin. He had just begun to scatter more snowflakes when the school bell rang, calling the children in from recess. In trooped the noisy youngsters. Recess never seemed long enough anyway, but with a new snowfall coming down, it would be harder than ever to concentrate on math and history.

Virginia watched the hands of the clock. Would they never hurry? The little group of students moved restlessly in their seats. The very air seemed to grow gray, and a chill settled over the room that the roaring fire in the old iron stove could not quite overcome.

Miss Sterns closed her book and looked nervously out the window. Instantly 11 heads rose and turned toward the sound of swirling snow striking against the windowpanes. The gentle flakes that had started to fall during recess time had become a fine, driving wall of white.

"Children," said Miss Sterns, "the storm is much worse. I am going to dismiss you right now, and you must hurry straight home. Don't forget your caps and mittens, and don't linger anywhere."

Soon the little church school was empty. Miss Sterns banked the fire and turned out the lights, taking one last glance around the room as she closed the door.

Miss Sterns was staying at the home of Virginia and Carol Haney. Every day she brought them to school with her, chauffeuring them and their older cousin Joe in the Haneys' family car. Miss Sterns thought of the long country road ahead as she got into the car with the children. Joe was a dependable eighth-grader and her standby when it came to cars. Virginia was a lively sixth-grader, and little Carol was just 7 and in the first grade.

As Miss Sterns was getting the car warmed up, Virginia's father came trudging through the snow. He had walked the seven long miles from the farm to make sure the little group got home safely.

The old car sneezed and coughed along, and at times it seemed as though it would be blown from the road. The drifts were fast filling the ditches and were beginning to pile up on the highway.

Suddenly, over the hill came the lights of two cars traveling very fast and side by side. Father turned the wheel, and the old car buried itself in the drifted ditch, just in time to avoid being struck by the on-coming cars. A quick check showed that no one was hurt, so Father and Joe decided they would dig the car out and try to get it started again while Miss Sterns and the younger children started walking.

They were a forlorn-looking group plodding through the drifts. Carol began to cry, the tears freez-ing on her little cheeks almost as fast as they fell.

"We must pray for help," said Miss Sterns. With bowed heads, there in the wind and snow, they asked God for help.

"O God, send our guardian angels," prayed Virginia. Grandma had told her that her angel would protect her, and Virginia felt that she certainly needed that protection now.

From behind them came the sound of a motor and the lights of an automobile. Drawing the chil-dren to one side, Miss Sterns picked up the crying Carol and waited for the car to pass, but the car stopped beside them. A pleasant-voiced stranger of-fered to take them home.

They scrambled into the car, relieved to get out of the cold wind. Virginia slid forward to the edge of her seat behind the driver. "I'll show you where we live," she offered.

Half turning toward her, he answered, "I know where you live."

Virginia settled back in her seat. The warmth from the heater made her drowsy. Presently she was startled awake by the lights of neighboring farms. The storm was over and the snow had stopped. As Virginia watched, the driver turned into the driveway of their home. The car moved along seemingly without effort, right up to the back steps. Miss Sterns and Virginia climbed out. The driver picked up the sleepy Carol and carried her to the door. Declining the invitation to come in, he turned back to his car.

Home and supper were most welcome. Everyone talked about the storm. A neighboring family stopped by for a moment and were very much interested in the stranger, for no one could recall having seen him before.

Later Dad and Joe came in with the old car. Joe went to bed early, exhausted with his efforts in the snow. Dad started for the barn to make one last check for the night when the family heard him calling from the driveway. His voice was excited, and Virginia ran out with some of the others to see what he wanted.

There before them stretched a single row of car tracks, tracks that came in from the road and stopped at the door but did not go out again. The car that had made them could not have left by backing in its own single track the whole long driveway without some extra marks showing in the new snow. Taking the lantern, the family examined the tracks closely from the beginning of the driveway to where the tracks ended so abruptly at the steps—ended as though man and car had taken wings and flown away.

Dad didn't puzzle long. After making sure that everyone was satisfied that the car had not left by any ordinary method, he said softly, "Only an angel could have done it."

My guardian angel! thought Virginia. *I prayed for him to come, and he did. I wonder if I'll ever see him again. I must remember what he looked like so I'll recognize him next time.* She snuggled down into the big feather bed.

The household finally settled down to sleep. Outside, the winter wind began its work of filling a set of tracks. Were they ordinary car tracks? Were they angel tracks? Who can tell? A child's prayer, a mysterious stranger never seen before in the community, and a set of single car tracks in the new-fallen snow that went only one way and stopped forever at a humble farmhouse door!

Part of a Bible verse struggled to make itself remembered in Virginia's sleepy brain: "Some people have entertained angels" (Hebrews 13:2).

12

Who Woke the Captain?

by Allen Sonter

The mission ship *Fetu Ao [Day Star]* rolled gently in the long swells as it chugged along through the warm tropic ocean. In the wheelhouse the glow of light from the steering compass faintly eliminated the brown face of the helmsman as he moved the wheel a little from time to time to keep the ship on course. The young man on watch peered sleepily ahead into the inky darkness, broken only by the shadowy outline of the ship's bow.

It was the darkest hour, the hour before dawn, and apart from the two men on duty the ship was wrapped in slumber. I was down in the cabin asleep along with Pastor Alec Thomson, captain of the little vessel. I had come on this trip to learn navigation.

We were on our way from Tarawa in the Gilbert Islands to Ocean Island, a small speck scarcely more than a mile across, lying 240 miles from Tarawa and about 60 miles south of the equator in the middle of the vast Pacific Ocean. As we had studied our charts the evening before Pastor Thomson had straightened up and said, "Well, we should see Ocean Island about 7:30 in the morning."

The sky had been overcast all day, and it was still overcast in the evening. That worried me a little, for we were unable to take star sights to determine our position. But Pastor Thomson had stilled my fears. "Don't worry, Allen," he said. "When the clouds come up and cover the stars we must be about on course. If the Lord sees we're going the wrong way, He'll show us the stars so we can check our position."

Now, as the hours of darkness slipped away on this last night at sea the hands of the clock on the cabin wall crept around to 5:00 in the morning. Suddenly Pastor Thomson became wide awake. It was as if someone had touched them. Sitting up, he peered around in the darkness of the cabin. Everything was still. There was no sound except for the occasional creaking of the ship, the gentle swish of the water outside, and the muted sound of the engines.

I'm sure someone woke me, he thought to himself, *but there seems to be no one about at all.*

Since he was awake, he decided to go up front and see that everything was in order. Stepping into the wheelhouse, he received a sleepy greeting from the watchman and asked how things were going. "Still on course," came the reply.

Taking the binoculars from the case, he climbed the ladder to the wheelhouse roof. The breeze felt good after the stillness of the cabin. He lifted the glasses and with an experienced eye scanned the horizon.

Wait! What was that? His eye had detected a faint glow off on the starboard (right) bow. Moving the glasses back and forth, he found it again. Yes, it seemed like a faint light. But what could be making a light out there? Ocean Island should be straight ahead, and in any case, it was miles away yet. We would not catch the first glimpse of it for at least two or three more hours. There were no other ships reported in the area, so it couldn't be the light from a ship. Perhaps his imagination was playing tricks on him.

Pastor Thomson climbed down the ladder and returned to the cabin. Shaking me awake, he said, "Come up on top and have a look."

A few moments later we were on top of the wheelhouse, and as I rubbed my eyes and steadied myself against a ventilator he handed me the glasses. "See if you can make out anything interesting," he remarked as I lifted the glasses and focused them on the faint line of the horizon ahead.

At first I could make out nothing, but as I moved the glasses around to the starboard side a faint glow caught my attention. "Say, there's a light over there!" I exclaimed.

"So you can see it too," he nodded. Briefly he told me how he had seen the light but doubted his own eyes. "There's only one thing it can be. It must be Ocean Island. We must have traveled faster than we thought. But what puzzles me more is that it's at least 30 degrees to starboard of our course."

"We had no star sights last evening," I said. "We could be that much off course."

After discussing the problem for a few moments we decided that we should alter course toward the light. I stayed up on top with the glasses while Pastor Thomson went below and took the wheel. Slowly the bow began to swing over as I kept the glasses glued to that faint glow. "That's it," I called as the mast came in line with the light and the ship steadied on the new course. Then, as if someone had thrown a switch, the light went out!

When Pastor Thomson joined me again I handed him the glasses saying, "It's gone. It was there until we set course by it, but then it disappeared."

He stood looking intently ahead for a long time before he lowered the glasses and shook his head. "I can't understand it, but there *was* something there."

Slowly and thoughtfully we climbed down into the wheelhouse. "Let's look at the chart," he suggested.

Spreading the chart out on the table, Pastor

Thomson measured the distance between our estimated position and Ocean Island. "We can't be less than 25 miles away," he mused, "and in any case, the only lights at this time of the morning are at the phosphate workings on the opposite side of the island, and they are hidden from us by a hill."

From our position so close to the water we knew we would not see the low hump of the island until we were within 11 or 12 miles of it, and with our speed of six or seven knots it would be two hours before we could expect to see land. The clock showed 5:30, and we sat looking at the chart in puzzled silence.

Finally I spoke. "Something made that light, so I think we should stay on our new course for a couple of hours and see what turns up."

Pastor Thomson agreed, so we climbed back into our bunks with a prayer in our hearts that the Lord would guide us to the island.

The first light of dawn began to chase away the darkness in the east. Over to the south, where we would have been had we not changed course, a tropical storm poured down rain in torrents, completely blotting out the sea. An agile Gilbertese sailor climbed precariously to the top of the mast searching the horizon ahead for the first glimpse of land. The excitement could be felt. When would we see land?

A little later as I stood on the wheelhouse roof musing over the unusual happenings of the early morning Pastor Thomson joined me. "I'm certainly glad we aren't over there," he remarked, pointing to the south. "We wouldn't be able to see land a quarter mile away." Then glancing at his watch he added, "It's 7:30 now, so we should see land any minute."

The words had just been spoken when from the masthead came the excited cry, "Land ho!"

Sure enough, within a few minutes we could catch glimpses of the island dead ahead as the ship rose on top of the swells.

"So the light did come from the island," said Pastor Thomson.

"Yes," I replied, "but how?"

After plotting our position on the chart, we estimated the course of the storm then passing to the south, and the mystery of the light became clear. The storm had been passing over Ocean Island about 5:00, and the light we had seen was the reflection from the underside of the clouds of the huge floodlight around the phosphate works.

"But why did you wake up just then?" I asked.

"It just seemed that someone touched me," replied Pastor Thomson thoughtfully. "Do you think it could have been an angel?"

13

Heavenly Soldiers

by Goldie Down

It was great to be home again. Twelve-year-old Leyla sighed contentedly as she bit into her roll of tough bread stuffed with savory greens. There was nothing in the city that tasted half as good as Mother's cooking.

The three weeks she had been away at boarding school seemed more like three years. She had missed Mother and Father very much. She had missed Grandmother and Grandfather, but most of all she had missed her little sister Nadeema and her chubby little brothers, Munir and Manoug. Now the three younger ones crowded close, looking up with wondering brown eyes, as between bites she told them about her life at school in a big Arabian city.

"We do everything to bells," Leyla explained. "When the rising bell rings, we all get up. When the next bell rings, we go to worship in the chapel. When the breakfast bell rings, we go to the cafeteria to eat."

"Do you have the same kind of food as we do here?" broke in sister Nadeema curiously.

"Yes," nodded Leyla. "We have Arab food most of the time—but it is not as good as Mother makes. And sometimes they serve us American food."

"I wish I could go away to boarding school," sighed Nadeema enviously.

"Maybe your wish will come true when you are a little older," Leyla said. "Now, how about showing me the new chickens old Moogie hatched out after I went away. I have only two days at home."

With shouts of glee the children ran off to find the old mother hen and her speckled brood. Sunshine and laughter filled their happy, waking hours and all too soon the two days had sped by and it was time for Leyla to return to school.

"Here's a bottle of olive oil for you to take back with you," Mother said, holding out the bottle full of clear, yellow oil. "It's from Grandfather's olive trees. He picked the olives and crushed them himself."

Leyla took the bottle and tried to stuff it into the cloth bag that held her change of clothes. It would not fit. Oh, *never mind,* she thought to herself. *I can hold it in my hands. Maybe it'll be safer that way.*

"Hurry, Leyla," Father called from the front yard. "The taxi's coming down the street."

It was only 20 miles to the school, but their village was not on a bus or train route, and no one in the little town owned a car. The villagers either walked wherever they wanted to go or paid for a seat in the old taxi that plowed back and forth between the town and the city. Often eight to ten people would squeeze into the vehicle and share the fare among them. Only the exceedingly wealthy could afford to hire a taxicab all for themselves.

But when the taxi rattled to a halt that morning it was empty except for the driver. Leyla looked up questioningly at her mother as she heard her father asking the driver, "Don't you have any other passengers today, Abdul?"

"Sure. Sure." The taxi driver nodded and grinned as he leaned over to open the door. "Let the girl sit in here with me. I have to pick up a whole family down the road a little way—five of 'em wanting to go to the city."

Leyla's parents hesitated for a moment. They felt doubtful about sending their daughter off alone in a taxi, but they knew Abdul well enough. He had lived near the village for years, his wife was distantly related to Emir next door to them, and his children sometimes came to play with Munir and Manoug. Besides, he had to pick up all those other people. Surely it would be all right.

"OK," said Father. "Get in, Leyla."

Leyla settled into the front seat with her bulky cloth bag on the seat between her and the taxi driver and the bottle of oil clasped tightly in her hands.

"Goodbye, Mother and Father. Goodbye, Nadeem. Goodbye, Munir and Manoug. I'll be back home at the end of the term."

Abdul blew the horn loudly, and with a jerk and a roar the taxi rattled down the road toward the city. Leyla sat quietly expecting at any moment to see a family waiting at the roadside for the taxi to pick them up. Instead one milestone after another flew past as the taxi sped noisily along the country road, and still there was no sign of the prospective passengers.

"Where are you going to pick up the other people, Mr. Abdul?" she asked innocently.

The driver turned and grinned. Even before he spoke she had a premonition of evil.

"Let's not pick up any more passengers on this trip," Abdul said. "Let's find a quiet place where you and I can have a little fun."

For a few seconds Leyla was too shocked to answer. It did not take her long to figure out that the taxi driver meant her no good. "I am a Christian girl, Mr. Abdul," Leyla replied, her voice full of fear. "I don't want that kind of fun."

"Come, come!" The man turned to wink at her. "Even a Christian must have some fun, you know. Come on, sweetie. Just a little kiss."

"No," Leyla shouted. "Take me to school. Take me to school at once."

"Won't kiss me, eh? We'll see about that, little missy," Abdul muttered as he pressed his foot down hard. He drove furiously, and soon they were in the city.

Leyla watched anxiously for any landmarks that would tell her when they were nearing the school, but she had been at school only three weeks and did not know her way around the city at all. All the streets and buildings looked much alike. How could she know which street led up the hill to where her school was situated? And the taxi was going so fast she could not jump out and run for help even though there were houses all along the streets. Oh, dear, what could she do?

Suddenly Leyla realized that the houses were sparser. There were no more shops. The wicked man had driven right through the city, and now they were out on a country road again, a strange road, one she had never been on before. What should she do? What would happen now?

In her desperate plight Leyla thought of prayer. She had attended Christian schools all her life, even though her parents were Muslims. She had listened to many stories of answered prayers, and she knew that God does answer prayers—other people's prayers, that is. Would he, could he, answer hers now and save her from this dreadful man?

Dear God. Leyla's thoughts formed themselves into a prayer. *Please help me. Rescue me from this wicked man.* Again and again the words raced through her mind as the wheels raced along the road.

"Come now, sweetie, just a little love." The car was slowing to a stop. Could she jump out and run? But there was nowhere to run for help. There were no farmhouses or huts nearby, not even a tree that she could climb.

Leyla closed her eyes to shut out the sight of the leering face coming closer. Frantically she cried out aloud, "Oh, God, please save me now."

The car coughed to a stop and Leyla tensed herself for a struggle—but the man did not touch her. What was he up to? She opened her eyes, then blinked and stared.

Abdul was sitting back in his seat with both hands clutching the steering wheel and staring fixedly through the windshield.

Leyla straightened up and looked through the windshield too. The road ahead that had been empty moments before was now a solid mass of gray-clad soldiers marching toward them; their own country's soldiers.

Leyla stared in bewilderment. Where had they come from? There had not been a soldier in sight when she had closed her eyes a few seconds earlier. It seemed as if the soldiers had dropped right down from the sky.

The officer marching at the head of the soldiers waved Abdul, motioning for him to turn around and go back. Certainly he could not go forward, for the road was full of marching soldiers as far as Leyla could see.

Leyla's heart leaped with joy. She was saved. She put her hand on the door latch and said aloud to Abdul, "If you don't promise to take me straight back to school I shall jump out and tell these soldiers what you are trying to do. They will take care of you."

Abdul scowled darkly, but there was nothing he could do but obey. All the bravado had gone out of him. "All right. I'll take you back," he growled.

He turned the taxi around toward the city and stepped on the gas. The rearview mirror on the cab was so dirty and cracked that Leyla couldn't see anything in it, so she turned around and looked through the back window. For as far back as she could see the road stretched behind them straight and bare and empty.

14

White Uniforms

by Sydney Allen

Thomas wondered whether it might be possible for him to lie on his back for a little while. His chin, stomach, and toes had been hugging the rough boards of the cafeteria floor for so long that he felt he simply had to change his position.

"Mr. Alden, sir," he asked, "may I turn over onto my back?"

"I suppose so, Thomas, but be quick about it."

Thomas didn't think it at all unusual to be taking refuge from gunfire. He had never known what it was like to live without war. He had grown up during World War II, and when that was over various guerrilla uprisings around his home had made him as used to the sound of rifle shots and whistling bullets as he was to the crowing of the neighborhood roosters.

He didn't complain, then, when he found that a

gang of bandit rebels regularly exchanged fire with the government troops stationed next door to the school. The sound of the guns going off just made things seem more natural, except that Mr. Alden insisted that the students lie down during the gunplay, although Thomas had never bothered to do this back home.

It was easy for Thomas to forget the hardships, because he loved learning the truth that Mr. Alden and the other teachers presented in the classes. Thomas loved to study the Bible best of all, and it had never escaped his notice that Abraham and Moses and David had also lived through times of war.

Thomas had come to the academy from Sumobo, an island far to the north, by means of canoe, boat, and finally a train pulled by a chugging, gasping old German locomotive that had frightened him more than the tanks and the fighter planes with which he was more familiar.

He had dedicated his life to becoming a preacher, and for that reason he was willing to work for the privilege of study—something that not all the students were willing to do yet.

Thomas had, in fact, made himself indispensable to Mr. Rawlins, the farm manager. Mr. Rawlins, you see, had learned the national language that was used in the country's schools, but the people who lived directly around the academy couldn't understand that language. Consequently Mr. Rawlins couldn't do business with them.

Thomas wasn't a native speaker of that language either, but he had made a determined effort to learn it. Now he contracted most of the business for Mr. Rawlins in the surrounding *kampongs*, or villages.

Most of the people in Bahasaland were followers of the prophet Muhammad. They knew about Jesus but didn't believe His gospel, and they were not always friendly to those who did. While they were amazed and pleased at the speed with which Thomas had picked up their language, they suspected (and rightly so) that he would use his knowledge to try to preach Christ to them, so they were usually a bit distant toward him.

One woman in the market at Jakarewa, however, took an interest in Thomas because she too came from Sumobo. She told him, from time to time in his own native tongue, that the bandits were planning to make a raid on this place or that. Thomas, in turn, always warned Mr. Alden, so that he could make sure the school buildings and all the faculty and students were safe.

She told Thomas one afternoon that a gang was going to try to extort money from a landowner near the academy. Thomas hurried back to spread the word.

Mr. Alden gathered the students in the cafeteria, the only building that was fully completed at that time. He led out in evening worship and went on telling stories about God's watchcare over His people until the firing started about 7:00.

Bullets whistled back and forth between the cavalry post behind the school and the bandit hideout down in the canyon in front. Meanwhile, all those in the cafeteria tried to make themselves as narrow a target as possible. Thomas hugged the floor.

The shooting finally stopped about 9:00, but Mr. Alden asked everyone to stay in the room until he was sure they were safe. About a half hour later the major who was in command of the soldiers rode over to say that no more trouble was anticipated.

Thomas was glad that it wasn't his turn to stand watch, because he had noticed that the major had not said whether or not the bandits had been captured or destroyed.

The school program went normally for about two months, and then something happened that chilled the hearts of the small number of people who learned of it.

Thomas was at the market trying to purchase some setting hens for Mr. Rawlins. He was unable to find any, so, although he hadn't planned to see her that day, he went to ask the woman from Sumobo whether she could help him find some.

"Have you heard the bandits' latest plans?" she asked.

"No; what are they?"

"They are out of money again. They have heard that Mr. Alden has a lot of *rupastres* [the local currency] in his safe up there, and they have decided to get them. You'd better warn him, although he probably won't be able to refuse the bandits when they come."

Thomas decided to let the hens wait for another time. He jumped onto the pony he used for marketing and raced back up the hill.

This was something new! Thomas and the other students had always assumed that the shooting was a matter between the army and the bandits. The possibility that the bandits might turn against the helpless teachers and students had never entered their minds.

"It may not be true, Thomas," Mr. Alden said, "and even if it is, don't tell anyone about it. We don't want to throw everybody into a panic."

But it did turn out to be true. Two days later Mr. Alden found a note in the language of the district slipped under his living room door. He called Thomas and asked him to translate it. Thomas read out loud:

"ALDEN, BLOND MAN FROM AMERICA: We know that you are stealing from our people. Bring 1 million *rupastres* to the Jakarewa market today or we will cut your throat from ear to ear. Signed, the FREEDOM WARRIORS."

None of the scary things that had happened so far

had bothered either Mr. Alden or Thomas very much, but as the two looked at each other they realized that this was something different. The very existence of the school was at stake.

"Well, Thomas," Mr. Alden said, "don't tell anyone about this. I'll notify the army major, but I don't expect him to do much about it either. He doesn't like our exposed position here on the campus. But at least I'll give him a chance to do his duty."

"But sir, don't you want me to deliver the money? I'm not afraid, sir. I'll take it down!"

"No, this isn't our money. It belongs to God. This is His school. We have no right to give God's money to bandits, no matter what kind of threats they make. God can take care of us just as He took care of Noah and Daniel and Paul. But be sure that you don't tell anybody about this note, please!"

Thomas didn't tell anyone until years later, after Mr. Alden had returned to his homeland in America. It wasn't easy, though, to keep quiet about it, and Thomas confessed to me that he had trouble sleeping for a while, because he thought that every little noise in the night must be the bandits coming to carry out their threat.

A week after the note was delivered, Thomas ventured down to Jakarewa to see about the hens Mr. Rawlins still wanted. He went to see his informant to find out why the bandits had failed to keep their word.

"Where did Mr. Alden get those soldiers in white uniforms?" she asked.

"Soldiers? White uniforms? We don't have any soldiers, in white uniforms or in any other uniforms. The men at the army post near the academy wear camouflaged suits, not white, and they haven't been surrounding the school, I can assure you of that."

"Well," the woman explained, "several people here in the market were supposed to get part of the money the bandits were going to take from your school. When they went to collect the money, they were told that a ring of soldiers in white uniforms had surrounded the school and the bandits had been given no choice but to rush back to their hideout!"

"Ho, ho! So that's how brave they are! Well, I'll tell you," said Thomas, "Mr. Alden said that God would protect us and our school and the money just as he protected the men in the Bible, and now I can see that he was right. Praise the Lord of Daniel and Noah and Paul!"

The woman was interested. "Could you get me a book that would tell me about those men?" she asked.

"Yes, I could," said Thomas. "I will bring it to you the next time I come."

"There must be something wonderful about a faith that makes a man brave enough to stand up to threats like that," she said.

"There is," said Thomas. "There is."

15

Stranger in the Dark

by Goldie Down

Hurry, Evaleen. Finish your supper and I'll take you to the bus. You'll be safe if you stay on it until it stops near your school."

Evaleen nodded and scooped up the last grains of rice and popped them into her mouth.

"I'll give you the money for the fare, and when the conductor comes around, buy your ticket and ask him to let you off at Lowry School. It'll be dark by the time you get there, and you might not recognize the landmarks."

"I'll know when I get there. The bus stop is right by the school gates."

"Yes, but things look different at night. I wish I could see you safely back to school, but I must hurry off to the evangelistic meeting as soon as I leave you at the bus. Pastor Down doesn't like his workers to be late."

Evaleen and her older brother Stanley lived in India. They were the only Seventh-day Adventists in their family, and that drew them close to each other. Since childhood Evaleen had suffered from a heart ailment that made her weak. She was naturally timid, and it was only after many prayers and much pleading that her father had allowed her to leave home and attend a Seventh-day Adventist boarding school near a distant city.

Stanley was training to be a pastor in the same city, and on this particular afternoon he had brought his sister to town to see the shops and eat supper with him. It was a great treat for the shy country girl who had only recently left home.

"Let's go. All the buses leave from Sivajinagar, and yours is number 38."

Brother and sister hurried down the narrow street, and Stanley pushed Evaleen into an already crowded bus just before it pulled away from the bus station. "Remember to ask the conductor where to get off," he said as he waved goodbye.

Stanley stood watching as the bus rumbled down the street and turned the corner to the left. "To the *left?*" he muttered. The bus should have gone to the right. Stanley had traveled that route many times when he was a student at the same school. Now he stood wondering why the bus had turned left when it should have turned right.

Like a flash the answer came. In his haste he had put his sister on the wrong bus! The bus that went past the school was number 38E. How could he have forgotten? How could he have done such a stupid thing? He rushed over to the nearest standing bus and shouted at the driver. "Where does bus 38 go?"

"To Marthahalli, 15 miles out."

Stanley dashed down the street waving and calling for an auto rickshaw. He leaped inside and pointed down the street. "Quick! Follow that bus!"

"What bus?" The driver revved up his motor and stared at the crowd that thronged the street.

"It went around the corner to the left. Quick! Follow it! I've put my sister on the wrong bus, and she doesn't know the city." Stanley was wringing his hands in anxiety.

They rounded the corner on two wheels, sending a huddle of dogs flying for safety and nearly knocking down an old man. There was no bus in sight.

"Hurry to the next corner. It may have gone around," Stanley directed.

The auto took off like a rocket and roared down the street, pedestrians scattering before it. The driver halted at the crossroad, and they looked right and left. There was no sign of a bus.

"Try the next one."

Again the little vehicle roared and bumped down the street and stopped at the crossroad. There was no sign of a bus anywhere—right, left, or ahead.

"Do you know which route bus 38 to Martha-halli takes?"

The auto driver shook his head. "Never heard of the place. It must be a long way out."

"It is." Stanley slumped dejectedly onto the hard seat. "Take me to the lecture hall on Mahatma Gandhi Road. There's no hope of finding that bus, and I'm late for the meeting already."

"O God, please take care of her," he groaned softly as the rickshaw rattled along. "I made the mistake; it's not her fault. Please get her safely back to school."

Beads of perspiration stood out on his forehead as he thought of all the terrible things that could happen. Young girls simply did not go out at night unaccompanied. Why, oh, why had he not checked the bus number? What if Evaleen landed at the strange place 15 miles away, in pitch darkness and knowing no one? "O God, please do something, do something. Take care of her," he pleaded.

Stanley performed his duties mechanically that night. He hardly heard a word of Pastor Down's sermon. His whirling thoughts were with a timid young girl on a speeding bus.

Meanwhile Evaleen settled herself comfortably on the leather seat and watched the bright city lights flashing past. What an exciting afternoon she'd had!

The bus had gone several miles and was in a dingy

residential area by the time the conductor reached Evaleen's seat.

"Single ticket to Krishnarajapuram, and please put me off at the stop nearest to Lowry School," Evaleen said timidly.

"What?" The conductor braced himself in the swaying bus and leaned down to hear her words.

"Krishnarajapuram. Please put me off at the stop near Lowry School."

"This bus goes to Marthahalli. Never heard of Lowry School."

"But don't you go by Krishnarajapuram?"

"Nowhere near. It's the opposite direction."

By now all the nearby passengers were turning around and staring at the nervous girl, and those farther away were craning their necks to see what was the matter.

"Then what will I do?" Evaleen choked back a sob of fear.

"I don't know. But you'll have to get off this bus at the next stop if you don't want to go out to Marthahalli."

The bus ground to a standstill and Evaleen tremblingly alighted. How dark it was! A streetlight at the next corner did little to dispel the lurking shadows. Fear gripped her heart, but before she could give way to tears of panic, a pleasant voice spoke.

"You seem to be in trouble, young lady. May I help you?"

Unnoticed by Evaleen, a man had apparently stepped off the bus. For a moment Evaleen hesitated. All the warnings she'd been given about talking to strangers rushed into her mind, but this young man's voice sounded so gentle, and he had addressed her in her native tongue. Besides, from what she could see of him in the dim light, he reminded her of her own brother. She somehow felt she could trust him.

"Yes. Oh, yes, please. I need help. My brother put me on the bus in town, but it was the wrong one, so the conductor told me to get off here. I don't know where I am, and I don't know how to get back to school." Swallowing back her tears, Evaleen told her story all in one breath.

"Where is your school?"

"At Krishnarajapuram. Right by the bus station."

"Then you will need to take bus 38E. It goes by a few streets from here. Come along with me. If we hurry, you can catch the last bus. The bus stop is several blocks away."

Evaleen followed the young man's hurrying feet up one dark street and down another until they came to a well-lighted main road. To her surprise, she was not even gasping for breath.

"There's your bus coming around the corner. We're just in time. I shall leave you now, young lady. I have a long, long way to go."

"Thank you. Thank you very much." Evaleen

took her eyes off her guide for a moment as she reached into her purse for a rupee to reward the young man. "Please take this for . . ."

She held out the money, but there was no one there. She looked up and down the road. Only a small boy leading a large goat was in view. The headlights of the approaching bus illuminated the road far ahead, but there was no young man there. There were no shops or houses nearby into which he could have gone. He had simply vanished from her sight.

Evaleen boarded the bus and sank into the nearest seat. As the vehicle pulled away from the curb, she leaned over the windowsill and scanned the street for a glimpse of the kind young man. There was no sign of him anywhere.

He said he had a long, long way to go, Evaleen thought as the bus rumbled along. *I wonder if he could have been . . .*

When Stanley heard the story the next day, he didn't wonder at all. "It was an angel," he declared. "God sent an angel to care for you in answer to my prayer."

16

Escape Route

by Bonnie Koncz

"**M**aria! Peter! Come to supper," Mother Miller called.

As the two children raced into the kitchen they nearly collided in the doorway. Laughing, they sat down at the table. Mother asked the blessing, and soon every plate was filled from the steaming casserole.

"Children," said Mother, "I have something to tell you. It's very important, and I must ask you not to tell anyone."

"What is it?" Maria asked.

"You know that our country has been taken over by another government. Food is difficult to get, and prices are making it hard for people to buy what they need, even if the stores have it."

"Yes," said Peter. "Uncle Carl's store was taken from him, and people who once owned their homes now have to pay someone else rent to live in them."

"That's happened to lots of people," said Maria. "I wish the enemy soldiers would go back home. It's scary to see them marching through the streets!"

"I'm afraid they won't be going," said Mother. "Life will never be quite the same. Even though things have begun to settle down, I fear for what may come in the future, especially as you grow older. That's why I've made my decision—we must leave."

"Leave our city?" asked Peter.

"No. We must leave our country entirely. Many people have already escaped, and others will be trying. I've prayed a long time over this."

"But, Mother," cried Maria, "haven't people been killed trying to cross the border? Oh, Mother! I don't want to go!"

Mother put her arms around both her children and held them tight. "Don't be afraid. God will watch over us whether we stay here or whether we go elsewhere, and I believe it is His plan for us to go. A man is coming to our house tomorrow to explain what we need to do."

Morning was slow in coming for the two children who waited to learn what their future would be. As the sun started to filter through the windows, Peter and Maria got up and dressed. They could hear the sounds of breakfast downstairs.

"Good morning, children!" greeted Mother. "Our

meal is ready." As they sat down to bowls of hot cereal and warm cinnamon toast, they heard a knock at the door.

"That might be the man," said Mother, "the one I told you was coming. Peter, answer the door. But don't say anything. Let him speak first. It's always possible that someone has discovered our plans. Even neighbors can't be trusted anymore. The government is rewarding those who turn in others as traitors."

Peter opened the door, and there stood a short man with graying hair. "Good morning," he said.

"Good morning, sir," said Mother, stepping up next to Peter. "It is rather early. Can we help you?"

"Are you—are you Mrs. Miller?"

"What is it you want?" asked Mother.

"My—my name—my name is George. I came to—Is there anyone else here?" he asked nervously.

"No, we are the only ones. Have you come to help us?"

After talking a few minutes they were convinced of each other's sincerity. The plan was laid out.

"I know the escape route by heart," he said. "A friend who has already crossed over showed me the way before he left. Three other people will be going with me, besides your family. We must walk to the border. Anyone in a vehicle would have to go on the main roads and would be more easily discovered."

The man shifted in his seat and then continued.

"Don't bring any suitcases or sacks, and don't carry any household items with you. You must leave everything behind. Come only in the clothes you are wearing, and a coat. You won't be able to bring any food along either. We must avoid all appearances of being on some type of journey. By all means, be casual. I will meet you at the edge of the forest near the water tower. On the other side of the forest is the border. We leave in three days."

As Mother closed the door behind the man, she looked weary. She had not anticipated leaving in only three days. The seriousness of it all weighed heavily on her.

"Mother? Are you all right?" asked Peter and Maria.

"Yes. I just want everything to go well. It will be hard, you know. It's a long way to the border, and we're not sure what we will find when we get there. We must remember every step of the way to be brave and have faith. Do you understand?"

Two nights later the frightened family prayed and planned together.

"Children," whispered Mother the next morning as she gently shook each shoulder, "get up. This is the day."

Quickly they dressed in their everyday clothes. Mother had fixed a large meal, not knowing how long it would be before they would eat again. She had the children wash the dishes, and while they were busy cleaning up, she looked around at the things she must leave behind never to see again. The family pictures, the handmade linens, the little mementos passed down through the family for so many years. It was so hard to leave it all behind when each little possession had a special meaning.

"Mother," said Maria as she and Peter came out of the kitchen, "couldn't we each take just *one* favorite thing with us?"

"I'm afraid not. Everything must stay, and we must go." With one last look they closed the door behind them.

They walked out into the street and began their long walk through town. "Try to be casual, try to be casual," rang in their minds with every step.

Mother greeted the baker who was standing in the doorway of the local store. "Good morning."

"Good morning. A nice day today."

"Yes, it is," answered Mother, hoping he would not expect her to stop and talk.

"Hello there," called a neighbor as she was sweeping her porch. "Come and see me later today. I'm baking a cake and want to give you some. I've been saving the ingredients for a long time."

"How nice of you," Mother called out.

Each person was greeted, and a word or two was exchanged as the three passed the familiar houses of their friends. *Why are so many people out and about already?* wondered Mother. After several blocks they no longer saw people they knew. But still Peter felt as if he had a big sign tacked on his shirt that said, "Escaping." It was hard not to feel self-conscious.

Some soldiers walked past on their morning patrol, and Peter thought back over the events of the past months. Resistance to the invaders had been strong. Civilians had fought alongside the military to push the enemy troops out. There had been fighting all over the city. Finally the enemy had withdrawn. The guns had been put away, and there had been great cries of freedom and victory. But they had been taken by surprise when the enemy tanks came rolling back, this time to win.

Mother is right to want us to leave, thought Peter. *And God will surely help us.*

"How much longer till we are out of the city?" Maria asked.

"Very soon, I think," answered Mother. "A few more blocks, and we'll be outside the city limits."

Finally they came to the forest. How beautiful it was. The autumn leaves had covered the floor with a crinkly carpet, and the bare arms of the trees seemed to reach to the heavens. George was waiting along with two other men and a young woman.

"Hurry over here," he said. The group gathered together for final instructions. "It is very easy to get lost in this forest, but I am sure of the way, so please do not get separated from me. I cannot come back for you. We must go as quickly and as quietly as possible. That won't be easy with these dry leaves, but do your best. There may be soldiers in the forest or people working, and I'd like to avoid meeting them. We'd have a hard time explaining what we were doing here. Now follow me. Make sure the children keep up."

As quiet as the travelers tried to be, the leaves made a noisy *crunch, crunch*. They stopped to hide a few times when rustling leaves told of the approach of a hunting party. Through the dense forest they wound their way—sometimes on the well-worn deer paths, sometimes straight through brush and foliage. It was hard and tiring hour after hour, but the little group was determined to keep going. Deep in the forest the incredible beauty made it hard at times for Peter to remember what a desperate situation they were in.

Suddenly George stopped. "I've changed my mind," he said quietly. "I can't go on. Continue on if you want to, but without me."

"But you can't do that!" exclaimed Mother as everyone pressed around. "At least tell us the way."

"I can tell you nothing," he said. "I have decided to go back. If you are caught and they find out who was leading you, it will mean my finish. I just cannot tell you," he cried.

The men began to argue with him, but he bolted

down the path and ran back through the forest.

"Mr. George!" Peter yelled and started to run after him.

"No!" said one of the men. "We can't go after him. He won't tell us anything, and I'm not about to turn back."

"But what can we do?" questioned Mother. "We have no idea which way to go!"

"We know the general direction of the border. And I think we are closer to the border than to the city. Maybe we have a chance."

"But we don't know where to cross over," said the young woman. "Without a guide we don't have a chance of coming out in the right spot. We're doomed before we try."

The older man agreed. But Mother, remembering her earnest prayer to God to guide her family, finally sided with the young man. Soon they were all in agreement to at least try, and off they started in the direction George had been leading them. With so many trees and such thick underbrush, it was hard to tell which way to go. For several days they walked through the forest, only to find themselves retracing their steps.

"We're going in circles," moaned the young woman. "We are hopelessly lost." Now more unsure than ever, they gathered together in a small clearing to talk. The wind blew and the leaves swirled around their feet.

"Mother," whispered Maria, and she tugged on her sleeve. Out into the clearing stepped two large men. They were dressed as woodsmen, and each had an ax slung over his shoulder. Mother knew that the men who worked in the forest were a rough bunch and probably wouldn't have much sympathy with what they were trying to do. At the very least, they would be robbed of what little they had. At the worst . . .

"I didn't hear them coming, did you?" whispered the young woman to Mother.

Mother shook her head.

"You are looking for the border, aren't you?" asked one of the men as they walked over.

No one said anything.

"We know you are. *You*. Come with us." They took the older man from the group and disappeared with him into the bushes.

"Oh, no!" cried Mother. "I'm afraid they'll kill him for sure. Why did they take him?"

"Let's run," suggested the young woman. "We have to try to get away. Think of your children."

Unable to decide what to do, they stood and waited. They didn't want to abandon the old man, who had suffered a great deal in their wanderings the past few days. In a short while the woodsmen returned, and behind them walked the old man with a happy smile on his face.

"I can't believe they didn't harm him," said

Mother. "I wonder what they want."

The old man hurried over. "They have told me everything!" he exclaimed. "We can get to the border for sure now. The way will be clear."

"But remember," cautioned one of the woodsmen, "don't try to cross over until exactly 4:00. That's when the guards go into their stations for one or two minutes to change posts and receive orders."

"How can we tell you how grateful we are?" said Mother as she turned to the man standing close to her. "I have a little money and a gold watch. Please take them as a small payment for helping us." She tried to press them into his hand.

The woodsman smiled and looked at his companion. "No, you keep them. We don't need money."

The little band of refugees hugged each and turned to thank their unexpected helpers. They could not see them in any direction. They heard no sounds on the pathway, no leaves crackling under their feet.

Following the directions they had been given, they reached the border a little before 4:00. The winter sun, now slowly disappearing, was casting its last rays of light on the wire fence that marked the border. Right in front of them was a hole in the fence. They took their coats off to make it easier to pass through. They knew that the fence, if touched, would automatically ring a bell in the guardhouse.

From their position in the bushes, they saw the guards in their towers, machine guns on their backs. At exactly 4:00 the guards left their posts and went inside the building.

"Now!" said the old man. As quickly as they could, each one scurried through the hole. On the other side Mother grabbed Maria's and Peter's hands and started running. The field was icy cold and wet, and the children slipped repeatedly.

"Keep going!" urged Mother. Soon she was half dragging them behind her.

It wasn't long before the guards reappeared. Shots rang out all around. Peter glanced down the field and saw other people scrambling to get across the border. On they went, running as fast as they could. Soon it was completely dark.

"Look!" cried Mother. On the far side of the field small lights began flashing, showing them which way to come. "We're almost there, children. Keep going."

Just when Peter and Maria thought they couldn't take another step, they reached the other side and were met by friendly faces. They were exhausted and cold, and their stomachs ached with hunger, but they were glad to be safe.

"God has surely guided us here," said Mother, and they bowed their heads together in prayer.

17

Ambushed!

by Holly Howard

C harlie's father, Dr. Jim, sensed a strangeness in the air as he stepped outside their humble missionary home into the burning East Pakistan (now Bangladesh) sun. His eyes scanned the nearby area. Everything seemed to be in order, but he still felt uneasy. Charlie and his mother followed him out of the house, carrying needed medical supplies for a village down the river.

Beads of sweat began to dot their foreheads as Charlie and his parents made their way down the familiar riverbank path. In a few minutes they reached the small boat, where the Bengali boatman waited with a long pole to push them down the river to the village.

Charlie stepped into the boat and took a seat in the front while his parents sat on the board under a worn, cloth covering. The boatman sank his pole into the riverbank and pushed away. As they floated downriver with the current, the day became quieter and hotter. Dr. Jim's uneasy feeling grew. Usually the river was crowded with people walking to the village, washing their clothes, or watering their animals. But today no one was in sight.

"I wonder where everyone is today," Mother said. "Is something going on that we don't know about?"

"I was wondering the same thing, Dr. Jim answered. "The river seems to have been abandoned. I hope nothing has gone wrong in the village."

Dr. Jim questioned the boatman, but he knew nothing because he lived even farther up the river than they did.

"Looks like something's ahead," Charlie said, standing up and squinting to get a better view.

Just then gunshots rang from the far side of the river. Charlie fell to the floor of the boat.

"Charlie!" Mother screamed as she moved toward them.

"Get down!" shouted the boatman.

Dr. Jim grabbed his wife's arm and pulled her down. "Stay here," he ordered. "I'll go." He slowly pulled himself to the front of the boat, where Charlie lay with bloodstained shirt and hair. He reached for Charlie's wrist, praying for a pulse. It was there.

"I'm OK," came a weak voice. "My ear hurts."

There was a bad nick in one of Charlie's earlobes,

but the bullet didn't seem to have touched him anywhere else.

"Try to relax," Dr. Jim encouraged. "I guess the recent truce between the two local tribes didn't hold."

"What are we going to do?" Mother asked anxiously. "We'll be killed if we don't get to shore." They looked back at the boatman whose desperate gestures indicated that he had lost the pole.

"Keep quiet and pray," Dr. Jim said, trying to sound calm.

Just then he heard a voice. "Take this rope, and I'll pull you to shore." A stranger in a smaller boat nearby threw a rope over the side of their vessel. "Stay down. You'll be safe," he said.

Their boat glided through some tall grass along the side of the river from which no gunshot had come. Several Bengali friends who had been waiting for the arrival of medical supplies met them. "Oh, we're so glad you're alive! We prayed for God to save you, and He caused the wind to blow you to us."

"But didn't you see the man in the small boat?" Dr. Jim asked. "*He* brought us to the bank."

"No, no, the wind—it was the wind. It blew you to the tall grass, to safety. We didn't see any man or boat."

"But—" Dr. Jim said no more. He bent down to help Charlie up, and his eyes studied the rope still draped over the side of the boat. "Thank You, God," he whispered.

18

Discovery on the Mountainside

by Elaine Egbert

I 'm not sure I believe all that religion stuff anymore," my cousin Alan called over his shoulder as he led the way up the steep mountain path. "Anyway, not the way Gram believes it."

I shrugged, but didn't say anything. Gram was a dear little lady who talked to God all the time, just as though He were a friend who'd come in for cup of tea and was sitting at her kitchen table. I heard her once when she was standing at the sink peeling carrots for lunch. It was as though she'd forgotten we'd come to visit, and she was telling Him how well her new pansies were doing.

There had been a time when I thought of God as a friend too, but since starting high school it just hadn't been the same. Not that I'd given God up or anything—I just didn't take everything Gram or my parents said and swallow it whole. And nighttime prayers were kids' stuff, I'd finally decided, and gradually forgotten about them, too.

Alan stopped and turned back to me. "Hey, cuz, do you think we should go on? I feel funny climbing in my Sabbath suit, and these stupid shoes sure aren't any good for getting a grip on the rocks." I laughed at how we'd look to anyone else, all dressed up and inching our way up a tough trail.

Ever since the family reunion had been planned for the Northwest, I had resolved to climb the mountain off in the distance. Today was our only chance because my parents wanted to return home sooner than planned. Since Alan was old enough to drive, Uncle Bruce had lent us his pickup truck so we could get out of the house and away from all the reminiscing. No one knew we had gone hiking.

I looked up the path to where it passed through a grove of young trees and opened into what looked like an old rockslide. The view from there should be good. I suggested we go just that far before turning back.

Alan agreed, and again we began plodding up the mountainside. At last we came to the opening, and though we couldn't see the snowcapped mountaintop from there, we could see what looked like a point a little way ahead—and from there we'd certainly be able to glimpse the crest.

We kept going on like that for an hour or more.

And at last we did come to a place where we could see the top. It stood tall and white against the blueness of the sky, and a wispy cloud looked as though it were blowing right off its face. I don't know how long I stood there looking at it. It was as though I'd forgotten I was with anyone, it was so beautiful.

Then my cousin spoke. "Hey, Vince, we'd better be getting back, don't you think? It's almost 5:00."

I shot a glance at the sky and for the first time realized how much the sun had moved. "Man! Much as I like it here, I don't want to stay all night!"

We laughed and headed back down the path, hurrying along until the trail forked. Alan stopped so fast, I nearly ran into him. He looked at the two paths and then finally pointed. "That's the one we climbed. But look how far it winds up the mountain and around the cove before turning back. It looks like if we took this other one it'd cut right across and we'd save a lot of time."

I glanced at the sky. The sun certainly wasn't waiting for us. "OK, let's take it," I agreed.

It was a good path, and though steep, quite easy to travel. The trees were taller, and the path curved back and forth around them and the great clumps of mossy rocks they sheltered. But at last we broke away from them and stopped dead still, mouths open, looking at what lay ahead.

"I sure didn't see that glacier from the path

above!" Alan croaked. "Look how steep it is."

My heart sank. I had read a lot about climbing and knew that crossing even a small glacier like this was dangerous, even with the right equipment. There was nothing else to do—we had to turn back, retrace our past hour of walking, and take the other trail. But by that time it would be dark. We'd be stranded on the mountain.

I looked at Alan and watched his jaw muscles work the way they did when he was thinking hard. Finally he turned to me. "Well, cuz, no use standing here resting our bones. It looks like if we stay on the high part of the glacier we can cross it OK. Looks sort of slushy, and it won't freeze solid again until sundown. But by then we'll be back to the truck."

I studied the glacier's steep descent to where it finally ended, dropping off into the sky. I gulped. "I think we'd better go back around," I said, trying not to sound chicken.

Alan looked at me, and I could tell he was worried too. "It would take too long. There's no way we'll make it home tonight if we go back. Think of how worried our parents and everyone would be. Why, they don't even know where we went, and neither does anyone else. There weren't any other cars down there when we parked, you know."

I looked down the icy drop-off and then at the sun, which had slid behind some low clouds. They cut out a lot of its brightness, making it look like a huge, round eye watching us. There was no choice.

"OK," I said, trying to sound more confident than I felt.

Alan started out onto the glacier, and right away I noticed he didn't seem to be having any trouble. Since the snow was a little slushy, his heels dug right in and he moved along quickly. I followed.

"Watch out for crevasses!" I called ahead, trying to keep my eye on my next foothold and watching for the dangerous cracks sometimes hidden in glaciers.

As rapidly as we could, we hurried across the snowy surface. For a while it seemed like all was going well. Then the clouds became thicker, shutting out all warmth from the sun. Already our feet were very cold. Our thin dress shoes were no protection from the iciness beneath. Alan turned back to see how I was doing, and he must not have seen the icy spot ahead, for suddenly his feet slipped right out from under him, and he started a slow slide down the hill.

Frantically I reached for him and lost my footing as well. Without meaning to, we'd left the slushy trail, and now the footing wasn't secure at all. We slid for only a few moments, but it seemed like hours. I watched Alan glide toward the drop-off. I wasn't far behind. "Sit!" I yelled as I flopped onto the cold surface and tried digging in with my hands. Alan did the same, and though that slowed us down a little bit, we kept sliding.

Frantically I tried to dig my heels into the snow, but I couldn't get a grip. My heart pounded so hard it seemed it would break right through my ribs, and still we moved toward the cliff. And then Alan got a grip on a small rock that protruded from the snow. He draped himself around it, and I made a mad grab for his jacket and finally stopped too.

Carefully we inched ourselves over so that Alan could slip his leg around the rock, and then I slung my leg around him and held on tight. It was pretty cold sitting there in the snow, and before long my fingers grew numb. The mountain had become an enemy rather than a friend.

We were quiet for maybe a minute. Then I couldn't hold my tongue any longer. "Now what are we going to do? There's no way we can climb back up."

Alan shook his head and mumbled, "And no way we can stay here all night without freezing to death."

We talked over several ideas, but none seemed like the answer. I kept visualizing the rock breaking loose and the long tumble we'd have to the boulders—and the river we could hear far below.

Finally I worked up my courage and made a suggestion. "Maybe we should pray."

Alan laughed scornfully. "Remember I told you I don't believe that stuff anymore? The way you've been acting, you don't either." He was quiet for a moment before he spoke again. "But don't let me discourage you. Anything is worth a try now. We don't have much choice."

I prayed silently, but I kept remembering the times I'd felt the urge to pray and purposely pushed it away. It was as though I'd been afraid my friends would know and perhaps make fun of me. I looked at the drop-off ahead and decided the time had come to put my fears behind me and make things right.

"Dear God, if You're there," I prayed, barely louder than a whisper, "please do something for us. Show us how to get off this glacier safely. And please, help the folks not to worry too much."

There was no answer. Then the wind began to below, and we could hear it whine across the smooth snow and moan through the rocks at the other side. The trees swayed, disturbed by its persistence. I looked around, trying to think of ways to move, and once tried to dig my heel in again, but it slid right out from under me.

"No use," said Alan. "We're here to stay. We'll just have to—"

"Hello! Are you in trouble there?" called a voice from behind us.

I turned so quickly that I nearly lost my hold on Alan. At the edge of the glacier stood a tall man, dressed in a bright red-and-black-checked woodsman shirt and jeans. He had a rope coil over his shoulder, and it looked like he was wearing heavy hiking boots.

We both yelled in answer to him, and before long

he had made his way across the icy slope to where we were. I could hear the cleats on the bottom of his boots bite into the ice. At last his warm hand grasped mind, and with the other hand he reached for my cousin.

"Now, just hold tight and I'll get you across. Plan your steps and don't stiffen up if you start to slide. That only makes it worse."

We concentrated fiercely on each move as he led us slowly across the snowfield, and at last we stepped onto the dirt pathway that rose sharply at its edge. I took my hand from his and brushed my hair out of my eyes, then started down the quickly darkening path. We'd really have to hurry.

Alan bumped into me. "Whew, what a relief!" he said as he grabbed me to steady himself. "There's places of me that are absolutely frozen stiff!"

I laughed shakily. I had the same problem! "Good thing you came along," I said, turning to thank our benefactor.

I couldn't have been more surprised if I'd suddenly found myself standing in the middle of Gram's living room. The man was gone! I looked quickly behind me along the path. Perhaps he'd started down, but I could see the trail clearly enough for a little way, and there hadn't been time for him to go farther. I quickly scanned the slope we'd just crossed, but it was empty. I called out and listened for an answer that did not come. And then it dawned on me that what had just happened was absolutely impossible. I broke out in a tingly sweat.

"Hey, I don't believe all this miracle stuff," I said, gawking at Alan. "But where did that man go?"

Alan's face was pale in the twilight. I could see his eyes darting around, checking every possible direction the man could have gone. He looked very sober as he clamped his big hand on my shoulder. "I quit believing that stuff a long time ago too. It happens only in mission stories." He shook his head as if to clear it, then shoved me toward the empty path.

We hurried along silently all the way to the bottom of the mountain, stumbling and picking ourselves up again. When we came to the bottom, we found the truck as we had left it, alone, no other tire tracks in the mud. We climbed inside, glad to be out of the cold night air.

But Alan didn't drive right off. He sat there staring at the windshield, unblinking and quiet. Finally he spoke, and his voice sounded full of gladness and hope. "But on the other hand, maybe Gram's right!"

And with a smile he gunned the motor and switched on the headlights. The two beams pierced the darkness, and with a roar of the engine we bounced down the mountain road toward Gram's house.

19

Camping
With Angels

by Kay D. Rizzo

We spotted the campground sign about five minutes outside of quiet little Las Vegas, New Mexico. "Do you want to stay there, or should we drive farther tonight?" Dad asked.

My sister and I groaned. *No farther, please,* I thought. After roughing it for a week in a national forest in northern New Mexico, my 10-year-old sister and I ached for hot water at the twist of a knob, showers that sprayed instead of spit, and real restrooms.

"I'm for stopping," my mother urged. "Tomorrow morning I need to find a laundromat so that I can do the laundry before Sabbath." Kelli and I grinned and clapped.

Driving through the almost-empty park, we chose a campsite on a knoll overlooking a small pond.

Except for one other trailer at the next site, the park stood empty.

We all helped to set up camp. Kelli and I spotted a playground not far away, and we were eager to explore it.

Just then a patrol car cruised by. The policeman waved at us, and we waved back.

"Mmmmm, hot water," Mom cooed as she bustled about the trailer's kitchen, scrubbing all surfaces within reach. "I'll have supper ready in 15 minutes. Stay near the trailer."

"Aw, Mom!" Kelli and I groaned in unison.

"Can we walk down to the edge of the pond at least?" Kelli asked.

Mother sighed. "All right, but come right back. I need you to set the picnic table."

Only minutes after we reached the water's edge and the cozy lean-to, Dad called, "Rhonda, Kelli, come on. It's time for supper."

As we ate, Mom noticed our neighbor removing the jacks under the corners of his motor home. "Isn't it quite late in the afternoon to be leaving the campground?" Mom asked Dad.

"I talked with the man," Dad replied. "He told me some motorcycle gang came around here last night. All the other campers left earlier today, and he and his wife have decided to spend the night in a motel."

"What do you mean? What happened? Is it safe for us to stay here?"

"Everything's fine, dear. The gang was reported to the state police, and the patrol cars have been cruising through here all day." With that, Dad continued to eat his supper.

After supper Dad suggested that we walk to the playground.

"You three go and enjoy yourselves," Mom said. "I just want to take a long, hot shower." Mom grabbed her towel, soap, and robe, and headed for the showers.

Kelli had a great time sliding down the slide, and I enjoyed having Dad push me on the tall wooden swing set.

All too soon Dad gave his last push. "Come on," he said. "It's time to head back to the trailer. Mom's probably ready for worship." By now the sun had dipped behind the rugged peaks to the West, and a rosy glow filled the sky.

Back at the trailer Dad said, "Kelli, please go get my Bible. We'll have worship right here around the picnic table."

I settled down on the bench, resting my head in my arms as Dad read.

"I call Psalm 34:7 the camper's promise," he said with a smile. "Do you girls remember it?" Dad began reading aloud. "'The angel of the Lord encamps around those who fear him, and he delivers them.'"

After the first five words, we all joined in. When we'd finished, Dad asked, "What do you picture when you imagine the angels camping around us?"

Kelli giggled. "I see them circling us as if we were in a wagon train, camping for the night!"

"I picture a bunch of little camp fires around a large circle," I said, "and angels sitting near them keeping warm, kind of like cowboys on the range."

Mom smiled. "Well, I imagine that the angels form an invisible wall around us."

"Or they can just be standing guard like sentries, every 10 feet or so apart," Dad added, posing as an armed guard.

Together we watched the last rays of daylight disappear behind the silhouetted mountains. Kelli and I crawled into our sleeping bags spread out on the bed in the rear of the trailer.

For a few minutes we lay silent, listening as our parents sat talking at the picnic table outside.

"What the people in the other trailer say the gang did last night?" Mother questioned.

Kelli and I crawled over to the open window to listen.

"They drove their motorcycles around the park with music blaring, shouting obscenities at the campers. Then they overturned one of the trailers. The owners had to get a wrecker out here today." Dad paused. "But everything's quiet tonight. The police have driven through the park twice since supper. Besides, short of sleeping alongside the road or driving all night, we don't have much choice."

I lifted the corner of the curtain to watch as Dad stood and walked over to Mom. "Let's take a quick walk." Turning toward our window, Dad said, "Mom and I are going to walk to the pond. We won't be far away."

Kelli and I slunk back down into our sleeping bags. *How did he know we were listening at the window?* I wondered.

A moment later I asked Kelli, "Do you want to play Uno?"

"OK."

I dug my penlight out of my clothes drawer and turned it on. Before long we were absorbed in the game. We didn't notice our parents' receding voices, nor, a few minutes later, the ominous growl of approaching motorcycles.

Ten fierce-looking cyclists pulled up behind our trailer, revving the motors on their giant black bikes and blasting their radios. Suddenly the thin sheet of aluminum siding between them and us didn't seem nearly enough.

I ran to lock the trailer door. Kelli jumped to the side window, scanning the horizon for signs of our parents. I hurried from window to window, closing all the curtains. What if the gang members tried to break in? What if they flipped the trailer on its roof with us inside?

Trembling with every sound, I avoided looking Kelli. I could hear sniffles coming from the corner of the bed.

"Hey, man! Let's have a party!" a rough-sounding voice remarked. Suddenly the trailer began shaking from side to side.

"Let's at least search it before we trash it!" another gruff voice said. With terror in her eyes, Kelli grabbed my sleeve and held on. We huddled closer to each other and peered out the side window. I was praying that our parents would come into view. Kelli was praying too. If we'd thought about it, we'd have realized that our 5-foot-11-inch dad could hardly have held his own against 10 streetwise bikers bent on destruction.

Just then Dad appeared with Mom following a few feet behind, slowly walking toward the trailer. Suddenly the radios turned off. Lined up at the rear of the trailer, the entire gang stood watching my parents approach.

"Good evening," my father began. "May I help you? Are you looking for someone?"

Kelli and I peeked out of back window in time to see a look of frozen fear sweep across the scowling faces of the bikers. Ten huge men in blue jeans, black leather jackets, red headbands, flowing hair, and beards stood momentarily confused—paralyzed. Then, as if they were being chased, they ran for their bikes and roared off in a cloud of dust.

With tears of relief falling, Kelli and I unlocked the trailer door and dashed across the grass to our parents' waiting arms. We walked back to the trailer together. Somehow we all knew that our adversaries would not return.

Minutes later a patrol car stopped at our trailer. While my father tried to explain to them what had happened, the two policemen looked at him uncertainty. What happened? What did the bikers actually see? What could have frightened them?

I won't know for sure until I get to heaven, but I like to believe that I know the answer already. I've heard stories about angels that were visible only to attackers. Could it be that angels, camping along with us, appeared to those bikers?

That night in New Mexico the "camper's promise" became very real to me.

20

Attacked in an Alley

by Mary Weiss Futcher

was so happy that I walked down the street as if I were floating on air. As a young Bible worker for the New York City Manhattan Church, I was having a fantastic day. Several teenagers with whom I'd been studying had made the decision to give their lives to Christ. I had one more call to make, but I wasn't tired. I was thrilled as I went to the next home.

I didn't expect it to take long, but it was after 10:00 p.m. before I left, again with wings of joy on my feet. Both parents and their teenage children in that lovely Jewish home had promised to be at church the next Sabbath.

My mind replayed the visit as I walked to the nearest subway station. I boarded the train without really considering that it stopped a whole six blocks away from my apartment. If I'd walked another block, I could have taken a train that would have taken me within a block of home, but I didn't realize my mistake until I stepped off the subway. No matter. I looked around and decided that the night was beautiful and a six-block walk wouldn't hurt me at all.

The subway had stopped where the streets weren't well lighted, but with a song in my heart I headed toward home. I thanked God for blessing my efforts that day and for being such a wonderful Savior.

Bible verses were singing through my mind when a huge hand grabbed me from the back and yanked me into a dark, narrow passageway between two tall buildings!

My mind raced, and it seemed that time stood still. I felt myself go hot, then cold. My hands were wet and clammy, my mouth dry. I wondered wildly what the man planned to do to me. Would he rob me? Would he kill me? I knew that people had been killed for a few cents!

I didn't have much money. My shoulder bag held only a Bible, several pieces of Christian literature, and a few other items, including my house key. I felt a numbness ripple through me from the top of my head to the bottom of my feet and realized with new terror that I couldn't make a sound.

Oh, God, save me! I cried silently.

In that instant the man dropped me as he would

a sack of potatoes and ran out screaming—*into the grasp of a policeman.*

It took me a few seconds to come to my senses, but at last I got up, shook the dust off my hands and clothes, picked up my shoulder bag, and went out to the dimly lit sidewalk, where the policeman was questioning my attacker.

"Are you all right?" the policeman asked me, deep concern in his voice.

I nodded. "Yes, yes, I'm fine now."

My attacker, held tightly by the officer, begged to be released. He was hardly coherent and kept saying that the lightning that had struck him right before he dropped me must have come from outer space. I pulled out some tracts and gave it to my attacker.

The policeman made the man promise never to do such a thing again, and then he seemed satisfied that it was all right to let my attacker go, but first he asked us to pause for prayer. As he prayed, the policeman mentioned both my name and that of my mugger. But at the time I was so upset I didn't give it another thought.

Later the police officer turned to me. "Would you like for me to walk you home?" he asked kindly.

"Yes, please." I was still scared, and I never thought to wonder how he knew my address. As we walked, he talked to me of the dangers of being in such a neighborhood at that hour of the night.

"God gave you a brain, and you must use it wisely," he said seriously. "You must think things out." He kept on talking as we walked. He spoke kindly but seriously, and with such tender love that I hugged every word to myself and have always remember his advice.

He impressed upon me the dangers of being presumptuous, of assuming that prayer would get me out of problems that I'd gotten myself into because I didn't use my head. At last we reached the lighted area of Broadway.

"Do you need to get back on duty?" I asked him, thinking that he had gone far off his assigned beat.

He shook his head. "I want to see you to your apartment door."

We walked slowly, and I told him about the people I'd met with that day, of the teens who'd given their lives to Jesus, of the family who'd promised to come to church. He listened carefully, obviously interested in my work and happy at the way God had blessed.

As I reached my apartment, my steps slowed. I saw the doorman open the outer door, nodded to him, then turned to thank the policeman for walking me home.

He wasn't there.

Puzzled, I turned to the doorman. "Did you see where the police officer went?"

The man frowned down at me. "Police officer? I didn't see anyone, miss. You came to the door alone."

As soon as I closed my apartment door, I fell down on my knees and thanked God for His wonderful deliverance. I could hardly sleep that night, thinking . . . and wondering. It didn't seem possible that I could have actually walked and talked with an angel.

The next morning I phoned the police station in my precinct and the one in the area where I'd been attacked, asking the name of the officer who had been on street duty the night before. Officers at both stations told me that only patrol cars had been in the area during that time.

Again, with great awe, I thanked Jesus for sending His angel to protect me.

21

Miraculous Misfire

by Barbara Westphal

The musty aroma of tropical plants invaded Juan Rivero's senses as the young literature evangelist walked through the mountain forest in a lonely part of southern Mexico. The great elephant-ear leaves grew down low, while the lianas, like ropes, hung from high branches to the damp earth beneath.

As he walked over the rotting leaves, Juan heard rustling noises that alerted him to iguanas and snakes slithering away. Sometimes it felt downright spooky in the jungle.

Is that somebody moving behind that tree? Juan's heart skipped a beat. Perhaps it was only a bird that had swayed the branches. Still, he had seen *something* move. Not only had he *seen* it, he had *felt* it—as though some presence was observing him.

God, he prayed silently, *I claim Your protection*

as I am out here doing Your work. Immediately a Bible verse he had once learned came to his mind: "The angel of the Lord encamps around those who fear him, and he delivers them" (Psalm 34:7). Juan determined to continue courageously until the jungle opened up again into civilization, where he could sell his religious books.

A few days later Juan told his friend about his feeling of being followed in the jungle. He halfway expected his friend to laugh. Instead the friend said, "I think your being followed is a very likely possibility. You know that family you are having Bible studies with?"

"Yes," answered Juan.

"Well, I just heard that their son has threatened to kill you."

"What?" exclaimed Juan, shocked. "But why?"

"He's angry because the family is changing their lifestyle so much. You know—no more *comiteco* [strong drink], no more pork on the table."

The young bookseller decided right then and there that with God's help he would try to win the friendship of the young man who was possibly stalking him. The next time Juan went to give a Bible study to the young man's family, the unhappy son was at home. Juan hastened toward him and threw his arms around him in a warm *abrazo* [hug], slapping the young man on the back, as is the custom between good friends. The young man, taken off guard, returned Juan's hug and smile.

Next Juan engaged him in conversation as if they had been buddies for years. Soon the young man was talking with Juan about hunting and fishing and local politics.

In just a few days the young man asked to join Juan's Bible studies. More amazing still, the young man asked to be baptized when his father and mother were.

"I have something to confess to you," he said to Juan one day. "When you first began to come to our home, I wanted to kill you. I was very angry. For days I followed you around. Once I was in the forest hunting and saw you coming down the path. Before you could see me, I slipped behind a tree and aimed my rifle at you."

Juan stared at his friend in disbelief.

"Then," continued the younger man, "I pulled the trigger—but nothing happened. I don't know what was the matter with my gun, for that very morning I had fired it several times. It had been working perfectly. Oh, please forgive me!" The young man hung his head in shame.

"Don't worry. Don't worry anymore," Juan assured him. "All is forgiven and forgotten. God was taking care of me that day. He saved my life so that He could reach you."

"Do you think so?" asked the young man with cautious joy in his eyes.

"I'm positive!" smiled Juan. "God not only had a plan for my life, but He had a plan for your life as well."

"Yes, you're right. My gun not firing was a *milagro* [a miracle], a real *milagro!* God was taking care of both of us that day."

The two young men smiled at each other and shook hands as Juan prepared to leave.

"Wait," said the young man. "Before you go, I have another question. Who were those two men walking on either side of you that day in the forest? I've never seen them around our village since then—and never before."

Juan's face turned pale—not with fear, but with the sudden knowledge that the great God in heaven had sent two heavenly angelic bodyguards to preserve his life that day in the humid jungle.

22

My African Angel

by Amity Pipkin

When I was very small, I thought angels appeared only to people in the Bible. But I don't think that anymore, because I believe an angel came to *my* rescue.

We were living in a small country in central Africa at the time. Vacation time had come, and my parents; my younger brother, Adam; and Ben, a recently arrived 19-year-old student missionary all piled into our old Datsun pickup to begin our jaunt. This would be the first time we could show a newcomer the wonderful wildlife to be found in an African game park!

After a word of prayer for our safety on the long trip ahead, Dad pointed the truck down the dusty, rutted roads and headed toward the border and the game park in the neighboring country.

After many miles of bumpy roads and swirling dust, I was glad when we finally crossed the border. Soon we could be setting up camp at the game park!

"Hey, kids, look at those ducks over there on the water!" Dad pointed excitedly.

There are lots of beautiful birds in Africa, but ducks are quite rare. So of course Dad had to pull over, get the binoculars out, and take a closer look. We parked near a bridge in the middle of nowhere, and Ben followed my parents toward the ducks. Suddenly Adam and I noticed armed soldiers emerging from the bushes!

"What's going on?" I asked Adam, trying not to show my fear. "They're talking to Mom and Dad and Ben."

We watched as the soldiers ordered the three-some to a bush outpost at the side of the road, where more soldiers continued to ask them questions. One soldier came over and told my brother and me to stay in the truck, so we rolled up the windows and locked the doors. Then we saw Dad, Mom, and Ben being marched into the African bush!

What if they don't come back? I thought, terrified.

"We should pray," Adam spoke up.

"Yes, Adam, we should," I said. "Dear Jesus," I pleaded, trying to sound brave, "please help our parents to come back . . ." I tried very hard not to cry so Adam wouldn't become more scared.

Adam followed with a prayer of his own. Shortly after we finished, a large truck came lumbering down the road toward our vehicle, rolling to a stop just in front of us. There were three people in the cab—two men and a woman sitting between them. It struck me as odd that a woman was riding up front with the men. Ordinarily she would have been perched precariously on the load behind.

The three people got out of the truck, but it was the woman who walked directly toward us. Her bright orange, yellow, and green *chitenje** caught my eye. She came straight to my window.

As I reached to open the window, my little brother pleaded, "Amity, whatever you do, don't open that window. Please don't open the window!"

His urgent begging caused me to hesitate, but for some reason I rolled down the window anyway. When the window was all the way down, the woman did something very uncommon for her culture. She took hold of my arm. I did not shrink away from this unusual gesture from a stranger in a land foreign to me. I immediately noticed that her hands were not hard and leathery like the hands of the local village people. They were smooth and silken.

"Why are you crying?" she asked in excellent English.

"Our parents and our friend have been taken away by the soldiers!" I responded.

As she stroked my arm, her voice was gentle. "Don't worry. They'll be back. Don't worry. They'll be back," she repeated soothingly.

The three strangers returned to the truck, and the hem of the woman's bright chitenje caught my eyes, burning it into my memory, as she walked away.

As the beautiful woman stepped up into the truck, I turned to speak to Adam. Before I could say anything, the truck's engine roared to life. I turned to wave to the woman, *but she wasn't there. Only the two men were in the truck.*

Moments later my parents and Ben returned, unharmed!

Although I can't prove it, ever since that incident occurred, I have believed that God sent a special messenger to bring encouragement and peace to us during our terrifying experience. And someday in heaven I intend to find and personally thank my African angel.

---

*Chitenje: a colorful six-foot strip of cloth wrapped around the woman to protect her dress.

23

Strangers Leave Footprints

by Ehren Howard

T welve-year-old Robert Cunningham sat by the kitchen window, watching a snowstorm raging outside. That winter in central Ohio in the 1930s had been filled with ravaging snowstorms and freezing temperatures.

Robert noticed the tall silhouette of a man in a dark gray work coat, almost obscured by blowing snow, plodding down the slippery road. The wind hissed with ice crystals. Robert could see that the man was a hobo, a homeless stowaway, one of many thousands who traveled on noisy, cold freight trains and spent their days searching for work, food, and warmth.

The stranger cautiously approached the back porch of the Cunningham farmhouse. Robert called to his mother, "I think there's another hobo coming. Are we going to feed this one, too?"

"Of course we will," she whispered kindly as she approached the window. "He's probably starving." She cleared her throat as a knock sounded on the back door.

"Yes?" Mrs. Cunningham began.

"Ma'am," he said, "I've been looking hard all day trying to find some work, but there just wasn't anything out there for me. I'm awfully hungry." He paused for a moment. "Could you maybe give me something to eat?"

"Why, certainly," she assured the stranger. She never turned anyone away. "Come in on the porch and have a seat. I'll warm up some food." Inside the enclosed porch the tired man put down his heavy wooden tool chest and took his seat.

While his mom was in the kitchen, Robert stood inside the doorway, shyly but carefully studying the face of the tall man. Questions whirled in his mind. *Who is this guy? He seems good-natured, and he speaks kindly. Why hasn't he found a job? Where will he go now?* The man's blue work overalls and coat looked threadbare and scruffy but surprisingly clean.

Breaking the silence, Mrs. Cunningham called to her son, "Robert, will you come help me?"

"Yes, ma'am," he responded. Soon they brought out of plate of steaming food and a hot drink.

Looking hopeful and smelling the steaming vegetables, the man said humbly, "I do appreciate this, ma'am." Then he bowed his head and prayed silently before eating. As Robert followed his mom inside, he thought, *This really is a good man.*

The night's howling storm began to quiet down. By the time the hobo had finished eating, the snow and wind had stopped. The man picked up his carpenter's toolbox and knocked on the kitchen door. "Ma'am," he said carefully, "you've done a kind thing here. I just want to thank you. I want to say—God bless you." With that he walked off the porch, around the corner of the house, and away from the porch light.

Wondering which way the man was headed, Robert walked out onto the porch. He stood and stared intently in the direction the carpenter had gone, then took a quick glance all around.

"Mom," he exclaimed, "there are no footprints in the snow. The stranger didn't make any tracks in the snow when he left!"

"What?" said his mom as she turned toward the door. She strained to see but could see nothing except smooth snow. Standing motionless in the dim light, they realized he was really gone. "Robert," she said solemnly, "that was no stranger. *Strangers* leave footprints."

* * *

When I heard this story from my grandpa Robert,

it made an impression on my heart. God wants us to care for people in need—homeless people, our families, and even new kids at school. No matter who you are, God's message is still the same: "Keep on loving each other as brothers. Do not forget to entertain strangers, for by so doing some people have entertained angels without knowing it" (Hebrews 13:1, 2).

24

God's Hero
at Los Piños

by Leslie L. Lee

Chickens squawked and pigs grunted under the bus seats. Passengers shouted, trying to make themselves heard. I could hardly bear the smell of the animals, even though the bus windows were open.

Glancing over at Pastor Reyes, I saw that none of this appeared to be bothering him. His face looked calm as he gazed out the window at the dry countryside covered with cactus and sagebrush. I wondered how he could do this day after day. I knew I couldn't.

As I studied the pastor's face, I noticed that soft wrinkles curled around his smiling mouth. His dark eyes shone with kindness. And yet his life of suffering and hardship also showed through. The silver streaks in his thick black hair and the weathered look of his small hands with their stubby fingers reminded me that he was growing older. His left foot was always turned inward on a leg that was shorter than the other one. *How can he endure the long distances he has to walk to visit his many churches?* I asked myself in amazement.

The bus lurched to the right, off the pavement, and bounced over some ruts. Clouds of dust rolled in through the windows, and passengers coughed. Finally the bus stopped.

"Bajamos aqui [We get off here]," Pastor Reyes instructed. *"El pueblito esta mas por alla* [The little town is farther over there]." He pointed off in the distance.

Peering out the window, I saw nothing except hills covered by cactus and brush. Grabbing the handrail of the bus, I swung to the ground. I tried to ignore the stares of the people looking at me—a 14-year-old blond, blue-eyed boy. They must have wondered who I was and what I was doing in their town.

I liked learning about the Mexican people and their country. Whenever I had the opportunity, I explored Puebla, the city where I lived and where my father was the principal of the American school. When Pastor Reyes invited me to visit a new area, I jumped at the opportunity.

"How far away is Los Piños [The Pines]?" I asked Pastor Reyes in Spanish as we watched the bus roar off down the road in a cloud of dust.

"About 10 kilometers [six miles]," Pastor Reyes replied.

In the midst of my wondering how he could ever limp that far, he interrupted my thoughts. "Let's see if that man over there will let us use two of his burros."

Picking up our sack lunches and our Bibles, I followed Pastor Reyes. After a few minutes of haggling over the price, we mounted the little animals and headed toward the hills.

I soon discovered that riding a burro wasn't as much fun as I had thought it would be. Its sharp backbone cut into me. I shifted my weight, trying to get more comfortable.

The burros moved steadily along the rough, rocky path leading toward Los Piños. Soon we entered a narrow canyon. Looking up past the steep cliffs, I noticed a lone hawk gliding silently in wide circles, searching for prey.

"The path is becoming narrower and rougher," I said as my burro dodged boulders on the canyon floor. "It feels like we're going up now."

"Yes," Pastor Reyes replied, turning to look back at me. "But soon we'll be out of the canyon. From there it's not far to the village."

Watching the pastor bouncing along on the burro, I thought, *Why does he ride through such rough county? Why doesn't he just stay in the city and preach to the people there?*

A while later we broke into open countryside. I spotted a wisp of smoke in the distance, curling from a chimney at our destination. We passed farmers plowing their fields and women carrying loads of wood on their backs. In the village Pastor Reyes slowed next to a woman carrying a tall jug of water on her head.

"Pardon me," he said, "can you tell me where we can find the home of Señora Maria Gonzales?"

"Of course," the woman said. "Do you see the end of this street? Just turn right, and Señora Gonzales lives in the third house."

Pastor Reyes thanked the woman, and we rode on.

As we tied our animals at a post in front of the house, a short dark-haired woman appeared in the doorway. "Pastor Reyes! How happy I am to see you!" she called out. "It's been a long time. You must be thirsty and tired. Please come into my humble home."

As I sipped a cold drink, I looked around the small room. The rough wood floor was clean, but the room had little furniture. On one wall hung two pictures of Señora Gonzales with a man I presumed was her husband.

After exchanging small talk, Pastor Reyes said, "Señora Gonzales, I must ask a favor of you. Will you go with us to your neighbors' homes and help us hand out papers announcing a series of meetings we are going to hold here in Los Piños?"

"I'd be happy to go with you," Señora Gonzales answered. "The people here are very friendly and will certainly be glad to receive your announcement."

All that afternoon we knocked on doors throughout the village, telling people about Jesus' second coming and inviting them to the meetings that would soon take place. Most of the villagers were friendly and interested.

Late in the day Pastor Reyes said to Señora Gonzales, "You have been very kind in working with us this afternoon. Now I have just one more question. How can I arrange to use the largest building in the village for the meetings?"

Señora Gonzales nodded and pointed down the street. "Walk that direction. Knock on the door of the last house on the right," she instructed. "That is the home of Señor Maiz, who is in charge of the village hall."

The pastor made arrangements to use the building. Before ending our day, we tacked up an announcement at the post office.

"Now we must be getting back to the highway," Pastor Reyes said. "The bus will be there in a couple of hours. We don't want to miss it." We mounted our burros and began the rough journey back through the barren hills.

As we rode back along the trail Pastor Reyes spoke. "I hope that through our visits and the posters, the Holy Spirit will impress people to come hear God's message. How wonderful it would be to have a Seventh-day Adventist church in Los Piños."

Although we didn't know it at the time, the village priest back at Los Piños was standing outside the post office looking at the poster. "What is this?" he muttered. The tall, light-haired man's face grew red with anger as he studied the announcement.

"Wh-what?" he mumbled in disbelief. "Religious meetings, here in Los Piños? We shall see about this. The mayor will help me put a stop to these meetings. No one except me shall bring God's message to the people of *my* village!"

Father Louis, the priest of Los Piños, hurried down the dusty street toward the mayor's home, muttering, "This is my village . . . *my* village! I've worked here for 10 years." He arrived at the mayor's home and knocked.

"Why, welcome, my friend!" Señor Diaz exclaimed, opening the door. "But you look pale and tired. Is something wrong?"

"Yes!" Father Louis blurted out. "Some preacher has come into the village and is planning to hold meetings in the hall. He must be stopped. We can't allow him to speak to our people!"

"Now, now," the mayor soothed, "calm down. Come in and tell me about it." As Señor Diaz led the way toward the living room, he added, "You know I support you. Together we'll conquer this problem."

The mayor's dark eyes narrowed in anger as he listened to the village priest's explanation of how Pastor Reyes and a young teenager had come into Los Piños and "stirred up" the people.

When he had finished, the mayor said, "Go back to the church and pray. I will call a meeting of the village council for 7:00 this evening. Meet us there. And don't worry; we will stop this preacher."

Later that evening one council member spoke for the entire group. "We agree—our people must not listen to this new preacher. Their ears will be filled with heresy and confusion!"

The village priest breathed a sigh of relief. "Then we must act. This Pastor Reyes said the first meeting would be held next Monday evening. He will be riding through the canyon. We can be at the top of the mountain and roll down heavy rocks on him. He will be crushed and so will his plans to preach to our people."

The council members nodded their agreement.

Monday afternoon Father Louis, Mayor Diaz, and four other villagers climbed through the brush, around the trees, and over the rocks to the top of the mountain. When they reached the top, the mayor spoke, "Let's stop here. It's a good place because the canyon below is narrow. When our rocks fall upon the preacher, he won't be able to escape."

"Quiet!" one man suddenly whispered. "I hear something." Peering into the canyon below, the group saw two people riding on burros.

"That's him," one of the men said. "And that's the American boy who was with him on the last trip."

"Let's push some of these rocks over to the edge," Señor Diaz directed. "When they're right below us, we'll drop them down."

The men leaned over the edge of the canyon, watching the two figures below and awaiting the command to rain down the rocks on them. Suddenly the village priest whispered sharply to his cohorts, "Stop! *Stop!* Don't do anything!"

The other men looked at the priest. "Look," he said, "there are soldiers walking in front, beside, and behind the pastor and the boy! We can't do anything or the soldiers will kill us!"

"Now what do we do?" Señor Diaz asked as the group moved away from the canyon's edge. "This pastor *must* be stopped from preaching in our village."

After some thoughtful silence, the village priest spoke. "Tonight we will attend the meeting. Perhaps the soldiers will have left the village by then, and we can put an end to the pastor and his preaching."

"But what if the soldiers remain?" one man asked.

"If the soldiers are still nearby, we will listen and then report that he is talking against the government. They will take both of them to prison, leaving Los Piños in peace once again."

That evening as Pastor Reyes began his sermon, there was a sudden commotion in the back of the room. I turned around and saw the village priest and some other men walking down the aisle.

"Get up and move to other seats," the priest commanded a group of people. The frightened attendees scrambled all over each other as they obeyed him.

What power he has over these people! I thought. *And who are the men with him?* My eyes caught the gleam of a machete carried by one of the men.

Pastor Reyes continued his sermon completely undisturbed by what had just happened. The eyes of all six men were glued on him as he spoke of God's love and his commandments.

Then I noticed the priest glancing around the large room as if searching for someone. I wondered who he was looking for. I learned the answer after the meeting was over.

The priest and those with him strolled toward the front of the hall. "Where are the soldiers?" the village priest demanded. "Are they in the room toward the back?"

Pastor Reyes' eyebrows arched upward. "Soldiers? I haven't seen any soldiers, have you?" he asked, looking at me.

I shook my head.

"You know what soldiers I'm speaking about!" the man said loudly, shaking his finger in Pastor Reyes' face. "The soldiers that surrounded you as you were coming through the canyon this afternoon!"

A smile slowly crossed the face of Pastor Reyes. He realized that God had sent His angels to protect us as we rode through the canyon.

"Friends," Pastor Reyes said, "don't you know that God sends His angels to be with those who share His message? Sometimes," he added with a twinkle in his eyes, "they even look like soldiers."

Suddenly the mayor rushed toward Pastor Reyes and me, madly waving a machete over his head. "Then if there are no soldiers here, no one is going to stop us!" he screamed. "Neither of you will leave Los Piños alive!"

Just then his arm fell to his side, and the machete clattered to the floor. Again and again he struggled to pick up the machete and to raise his arm, but he found himself unable to do so.

Turning to the priest, Señor Diaz asked in a panicky voice, "What's happening? Where does this preacher get his power?"

The village priest hesitated, then spoke slowly. "I do not know. But if angels surround him, God must be speaking *through* him. We will come every night to hear his words."

The next evening Father Louis, Señor Diaz, the other four men, and all the people of Los Piños filled the hall to hear Pastor Reyes' message. They came the next night and each night thereafter.

When the series of meetings was over, the priest,

the mayor, the village council members, and many others in the village joined the baptismal class. That was the beginning of the Seventh-day Adventist church in Los Piños.

Later, as we rode out of Los Piños on our burros, I understood why Pastor Reyes endured rough rides over rocky trails, and how he could stand with unwavering courage in the face of death. Long before, he had learned the simple truth that "with God all things are possible" (Matthew 19:26).